GOOD OLD-FASHIONED
SUMMERTIME
PUDDINGS

GOOD OLD-FASHIONED
SUMMERTIME
PUDDINGS

Sara Paston-Williams

National Trust

First published in the United Kingdom in 2010 by
National Trust Books
10 Southcombe Street
London
W14 0RA

An imprint of Anova Books Company Ltd

Recipes sourced from *Good Old-Fashioned Puddings*, published by National Trust Books 2007

The moral rights of the author have been asserted.

ISBN: 9781905400928

A CIP catalogue record for this book is available from the British Library.

18 17 16 15 14 13 12 10
10 9 8 7 6 5 4 3 2 1

Reproduction by Dot Gradations Ltd, UK
Printed by Toppan Leefung Printing Ltd, China

This book can be ordered direct from the publisher at the website www.anovabooks.com,
or try your local bookshop. Also available at National Trust shops and www.nationaltrustbooks.co.uk.

CONTENTS

INTRODUCTION   6

CONVERSIONS   8

AMERICAN EQUIVALENTS   9

PASTRY RECIPES   10

FRUITY PUDDINGS   12

CREAMY PUDDINGS   44

ICE CREAMS   62

COLD PIES, TARTS AND FLANS   76

SAUCES   88

INDEX   96

INTRODUCTION

The British tradition for delicious puddings is centuries old. Puddings – pies, trifles, fools, junkets, flummeries, fritters and tarts – have all been served regularly since medieval times. From the earliest recipes, through elaborate Elizabethan and Stuart confections to the elegant 18th- and substantial 19th-century puddings, a tradition has evolved which is an integral part of Britain's culinary heritage.

Pudding is the dish we have always done better than anyone else. They were a staple filler for the poor or a sophisticated delight for the rich.

Appreciating the British pudding is nothing new. When François Misson came here 300 years ago his admiration was unstinted: 'They bake them in an oven, they boil them 50 several ways: BLESSED BE HE THAT INVENTED PUDDING, for it is a manna that hits the palates of all sorts of people.'

Originally, puddings such as brightly coloured spiced jellies, flummeries, syllabubs, various tarts, custards, junkets and fruit dishes formed part of a second or third course of a meal, served alongside chicken and fish dishes. A typical second course might consist of veal, sweetbreads, lobster, apricot tart and, in the middle of the table, a pyramid of syllabubs and jellies. In Tudor and Stuart times a special course of sweetmeats known as a 'banquet' became fashionable among the rich. This evolved into our dessert course.

The enormous variety of puddings and the rapidity with which they were developed in the 17th and 18th centuries, as sugar became cheaper and more available to everyone, show that they filled a real need in the British people's diet – rich in fat and carbohydrates to keep out the cold, and in sugar and fruit to build up energy. The puddings of country folk were often made from meal of cheaper local grains such as oats and barley rather than wheat, but they were just as satisfying.

British cooking has always been influenced by its monarchs and our puddings are no exception. Elizabeth I received annually 'a great pye of quinces, oringed' from her master of the pastry at New Year celebrations. George I was known as 'Pudding George' and is probably the Georgie Porgie mentioned in the well-known nursery rhyme. He, followed by George II and III, loved fattening, suety boiled puddings and dumplings which were devoured all over the kingdom. It was also quite common to see plum duffs and currant dumplings being sold in the streets of London for a halfpenny each.

With the French Revolution came a great transformation in British cooking. Many French chefs fled to Britain and a change of fashion in court circles resulted in the vogue for employing them. Antonin Carême, who worked for the Emperor Napoleon, was lured to Britain to work for the Prince Regent. Queen Victoria employed a number of French chefs, the most famous being Francatelli, who created puddings that we still know – Queen's Pudding, Her Majesty's Pudding, Empress Pudding and Albert Pudding. This fashion was soon copied by a growing and increasingly prosperous middle class who, socially aspiring, encouraged their cooks to make French dishes or, failing that, simply to give French names to traditional British ones. Many of the most delicious and subtle puddings of Georgian times were temporarily forgotten, giving way to rather heavy nursery-style puddings influenced by the German taste of Prince Albert.

Growing literacy had a tremendous influence on cookery. It allowed people, especially women, to write down their favourite recipes, including regional dishes. Many of the traditional pudding recipes were preserved in rural areas, particularly in the large country houses. In towns, speciality restaurants, gentlemen's clubs and the grill rooms of the more exclusive hotels continued to serve truly British puddings, so that many recipes have survived, although not always in their original form. In recent years, British food has enjoyed a well-deserved revival, with more and more hotels and restaurants serving our great national dishes and regional specialities. Puddings are a great attraction. Although some are inclined to be rich and fattening, there is froth and lightness in abundance. Many regard the pudding as nutritionally incorrect – nice, yes, but excessively naughty. But puddings are not about calories or cholesterol, they are about enjoyment and pleasure. If Brillat-Savarin's last words really were 'Bring on the dessert, I think I am about to die', how right he was.

NOTE:
If you want to be a little less indulgent, yoghurt and crème fraîche can be used instead of cream in most recipes, or half and half.

VEGETARIAN ALTERNATIVES:
Vegetarian suet and the vegetarian equivalent of lard can be used wherever a recipe includes suet or lard. In fact, I prefer to use vegetarian suet as it gives a lighter finish. Vegetarian setting agents can also be used in place of gelatine, though you must follow the manufacturer's instructions closely.

CONVERSIONS

Weight	Liquid measure	Length	Temperature
15g (½oz)	15ml (½fl oz)	5mm (¼in)	110°C, 225°F, gas mark ¼
25g (1oz)	30ml (1fl oz)	1cm (½in)	120°C, 250°F, gas mark ½
40g (1½oz)	50ml (2fl oz)	1.5cm (⅝in)	140°C, 275°F, gas mark 1
55g (2oz)	75ml (2½fl oz)	2cm (¾in)	150°C, 300°F, gas mark 2
70g (2½oz)	100ml (3½fl oz)	2.5cm (1in)	160°C, 325°F, gas mark 3
85g (3oz)	125ml (4fl oz)	5cm (2in)	180°C, 350°F, gas mark 4
100g (3½oz)	150ml (5fl oz or ¼ pint)	7cm (2¾in)	190°C, 375°F, gas mark 5
115g (4oz)	200ml (7fl oz or ½ pint)	9cm (3½in)	200°C, 400°F, gas mark 6
125g (4½oz)	250ml (9fl oz)	10cm (4in)	220°C, 425°F, gas mark 7
140g (5oz)	300ml (10fl oz or ½ pint)	13cm (5in)	230°C, 450°F, gas mark 8
150g (5½oz)	350ml (12fl oz)	15cm (6in)	240°C, 475°F, gas mark 9
175g (6oz)	400ml (14fl oz)	18cm (7in)	
200g (7oz)	425ml (15fl oz or ¾ pint)	20cm (8in)	
225g (8oz)	500ml (18fl oz)	23cm (9in)	
250g (9oz)	600ml (20fl oz or 1 pint)	25cm (10in)	
300g (10½oz)		28cm (11in)	
350g (12oz)		30cm (12in)	
375g (13oz)			
400g (14oz)			
425g (15oz)			
450g (1lb)			
675g (1½lb)			
900g (2lb)			

AMERICAN EQUIVALENTS

Dry measures			
I US cup	50g	(¾oz)	breadcrumbs; cake crumbs
I US cup	85g	(3oz)	porridge or rolled oats
I US cup	90g	(3¼oz)	ground almonds; shredded coconut
I US cup	100g	(3½oz)	roughly chopped walnuts and other nuts; icing sugar; cocoa; drinking chocolate; flaked almonds; grated Cheddar cheese
I US cup	150g	(5½oz)	white flour; currants; rice flour; muesli; cornflour; chopped dates
I US cup	175g	(6oz)	wholemeal flour; oatmeal; raisins; sultanas; dried apricots; mixed candied peel
I US cup	200g	(7oz)	caster sugar; soft brown sugar; demerara sugar; rice; glacé cherries; semolina; chopped figs or plums
I US cup	225g	(8oz)	granulated sugar; curd cheese; cream cheese
I US cup	300g	(10½oz)	mincemeat; marmalade; jam
I US cup	350g	(12oz)	golden syrup; black treacle

Liquid measures		
⅛ US cup	30ml	(1fl oz)
¼ US cup	50ml	(2fl oz)
½ US cup	125ml	(4fl oz)
I US cup	250ml	(9fl oz)
1¼ US cups	300ml	(10fl oz)
1¾ US cups	425ml	(15fl oz)
2 US cups	500ml	(18fl oz)
2½ US cups	600ml	(20fl oz)

Measures for fats		
¼ stick	25g	(1oz)
I stick	100g	(3½oz)
(½ US cup)		

PASTRY RECIPES

SHORTCRUST PASTRY

450g (1lb) plain flour, sifted
A pinch of salt
100g (4oz) butter, softened
100g (4oz) lard, softened
3–4 tablespoons cold water

Mix together the flour and salt. Cut the fats into small pieces and rub into the flour until the mixture resembles fine breadcrumbs. Gradually add enough water, mixing with a fork, to give a stiff, but pliable dough. Knead lightly for a few minutes until smooth. Wrap in clingfilm or a plastic bag and chill for at least 15 minutes before using.

RICH SHORTCRUST PASTRY

450g (1lb) plain flour, sifted
A good pinch of salt
350g (12oz) butter, softened
2 egg yolks
4 teaspoons caster sugar
3–4 tablespoons cold water

Mix together the flour and salt. Rub in the butter until the mixture resembles breadcrumbs. Make a well in the middle, add the egg yolks and sugar and mix with a round-bladed knife. Add enough of the water, a little at a time, to give a stiff but pliable dough. Knead lightly until smooth. Wrap in cling film or a plastic bag and chill for at least 15 minutes before using.

PUFF PASTRY

450g (1lb) plain flour, sifted
1 teaspoon salt
450g (1lb) butter, softened
1 teaspoon lemon juice
75–100ml (3–4fl oz) iced water

Mix together the flour and salt. Add 50g (2oz) of the butter, cut into small pieces, and rub into the flour until the mixture resembles fine breadcrumbs. Add the lemon juice and enough water to give a soft dough, similar to the consistency of butter. Knead lightly until really smooth. In a clean linen cloth, shape the remaining butter into a rectangle. On a lightly floured board, roll out the pastry to a rectangle slightly wider than the rectangle of butter and about twice its length. Place the butter on one half of the pastry and fold the other half over. Press the edges together with a rolling pin. Leave in a cool place for 15 minutes to allow the butter to harden slightly. Roll out the pastry to a long strip three times its original length, but keeping the width the same. The corners should be square, the sides straight and the thickness even. The butter must not break through the dough. Fold the bottom third up and the top third down, press the edges together with a rolling pin and then put inside a well-oiled plastic bag and chill for 30 minutes. Place the dough on the floured board with the folded edges to your right and left, and roll out into a long strip as before. Fold again into three and chill for a further 30 minutes. Repeat this process four times more and chill for 30 minutes before using.

This is best made over two days, rolling three times and chilling overnight before completing the rolling the following day.

FRUITY PUDDINGS

New varieties of apple and pear were introduced from France in the Middle Ages. Other known garden or orchard fruit trees were plums, damsons, medlars, quinces and mulberries. Strange and exotic fruits like lemons, Seville oranges, pomegranates, raisins, currants, prunes, figs and dates had begun to arrive in Britain from southern Europe. These, particularly the dried fruits, were eaten in considerable quantities by the wealthy. The poor ate them on festive occasions, such as Christmas. At this time fresh fruit was regarded as bad for the digestion, so most fruits were roasted, baked or stewed in pottages.

The 16th century saw an upsurge of interest in fruit and fruit growing. Landowners began to turn their attention to horticulture, and their gardeners were kept busy developing new varieties of fruit and vegetables. Market gardening proved lucrative, especially around London, and Covent Garden was established as the City's fruit market. A wide range of fruits was being grown in southern and midland England. Further north, the climate imposed limitations and fruit was raised principally in the gardens of the gentry. There were parts of north-west England where even apples and plums were hardly known among ordinary people before the 18th century. In Scotland too, fruit was grown on a limited scale.

The medieval fear of uncooked fruit died hard and it was often blamed when a person fell ill suddenly. All through the 16th and 17th centuries, the best way to eat fruit was to cook it first with sugar and spices. Apples, pears and quinces were baked for several hours in pies. Soft fruits were boiled and pulped to form 'tartstuff' for pies and tarts or to be mixed with cream in a fool or similar creamy dish. These cooked fruits became an ingredient of puddings and were preserved so that they could be used all year round. It was only in the 18th century that fresh fruit began to be regarded as a safe and even healthy food, and its popularity has gone from strength to strength.

Jelly was particularly fashionable in the 17th century in making extremely decorative dishes and tableaux – fish swimming in ponds of jelly, birds flying in skies of jelly, great mounds of fresh fruit set in jelly and layers of almonds, raisins and candied fruits glistening through clear jelly. Usually they were highly coloured – even blue – and highly spiced. Wine jellies were very popular and later, jellies were flavoured with lemon juice, grape juice, bitter oranges or quinces. Jellies were stiffened originally with calves' feet or neatsfoot, later with hartshorn.

BUTTER'D ORANGES

Custard made with butter and eggs was a popular pudding during the 17th and 18th centuries. This recipe is more like an orange cheese or curd rather than a custard. It is very rich but also refreshing.

Thinly pared rind of 2 oranges
Juice of 1 orange
1 tablespoon concentrated
    orange juice
50g (1¾oz) caster sugar
4 egg yolks
3 egg whites
225g (8oz) unsalted butter
1 large piece candied orange
    peel
150ml (¼ pint) whipping cream
Slices of fresh orange

Serves 6

Put the orange rind in a small saucepan of boiling water and boil for 20 minutes or until soft. Drain and purée the rind in a blender or pass through a food mill, or just pound the orange rind with a rolling pin. Add orange juice and sugar to the peel and beat until the sugar has dissolved. Add the egg yolks and egg whites and whisk until the mixture is thick and smooth. Melt the butter and leave until cool, but not beginning to harden. Pour the butter in a steady stream into the egg and orange mixture and blend in a liquidizer for about 3 minutes, or beat with a rotary whisk for about 10 minutes. Refrigerate, beating occasionally until thick and beginning to set. Cut the candied orange rind into tiny pieces, or shred with a grater. Fold into the half-set orange custard. Pour into individual glasses or custard pots and chill well. Decorate, before serving, with whipped cream and orange slices.

BOODLES ORANGE FOOL

A speciality at Boodles Club in St James' Street, London, which was founded in 1762. It sounds simple, but is delicious. The idea of combining sponge with fruit fool dates back to the 18th-century version with ratafias.

4 trifle sponge cakes
Grated rind and juice of
    1 lemon
Grated rind and juice of
    2 oranges
55–85g (2–3oz) caster sugar
600ml (1 pint) double cream
Crystallized orange slices
Crystallized angelica

Serves 4–6

Cut the sponge cakes into 1cm (½in) strips and line the base of a glass serving dish, or individual glass dishes. Mix the rind and juice of the fruit with the sugar and stir until dissolved. Whip half the cream until thick but not stiff, and beat the juice into the cream slowly. Taste for sweetness. Spoon over the sponge cakes and chill thoroughly for 2–3 hours, until the juice has soaked into the sponge and the cream has set. Whip the remaining cream until stiff, and pipe on top of the pudding to decorate. Decorate with crystallized orange slices and angelica.

FINE ORANGE FLUMMERY

Flummery, a lovely pale slippery pudding related to syllabub and custard, is a delicious pure white jelly. In medieval times, cereals such as rice, oats or sago were cooked long and slowly with milk and flavourings. This was really the beginning of the flummery. In Tudor and Stuart times it became a much richer dish of cream flavoured with spices, orange-flower water, rose-water, almonds or wine, set with calves' feet or isinglass. It was often coloured and eaten in the second course with cream or wine poured over. For special occasions, it was made in the most elaborate moulds for 'set-piece dishes', such as flummery fish in a pond of jelly, or flummery eggs in a hen's nest of shredded lemon peel set in jelly.

Flummery is now easily set with gelatine and should be made in the most attractive mould you can find. It is still possible to pick up fairly cheaply elaborate Victorian china and glass jelly moulds in antique and junk shops. If possible, this dish should be made the day before you want to serve it.

600ml (1 pint) double cream
50g (1¾oz) caster sugar
Grated rind and juice of 2
    oranges
1 tablespoon orange-flower
    water
3 tablespoons warm water
15g (½oz) gelatine
Soft fruit and whipped cream
    to serve

Serves 6

Put the cream, sugar, orange rind and juice and orange-flower water in a heavy saucepan and heat very gently until the sugar is completely dissolved and the cream is just coming to the boil. Leave on one side to cool.

Put warm water into a cup and sprinkle the gelatine over the top. Stand the cup in a pan of water and heat gently, stirring, until the gelatine has dissolved. Pour through a warmed sieve into the cream mixture. Stir well. Pour into a wetted mould and leave to cool. Refrigerate overnight.

To turn out, dip the mould quickly in hot water. Serve chilled with a bowl of soft fruit and whipped cream.

FINE ORANGE AND MADEIRA FLUMMERY

This variation uses a splash of Madeira to liven it up.

ALTERNATIVE INGREDIENT:
1 tablespoon Madeira or
   sweet sherry

Prepare the flummery as instructed opposite but substitute the orange-flower water with Madeira or sweet sherry. Continue to make as before.

ALMOND FLUMMERY

Flummery also tastes delicious made with almonds.

ALTERNATIVE INGREDIENTS:
115g (4oz) ground almonds
4–5 drops almond essence

Make as before, but omit the orange-flower water, orange rind and juice. Replace with the ground almonds and almond essence.

LEMON SOLID

This pudding's ancestor was the posset, but instead of being thickened with breadcrumbs, eggs and almond-flavoured biscuit crumbs, or ground almonds, were used. Lemon Solid is found in varying forms in many old cookery books and is one of the glories of British cooking, despite its rather uninspiring name.

600ml (1 pint) thick
   double cream
Grated rind and juice of
   2 lemons
115g (4oz) caster sugar
3–4 macaroons, homemade
   if possible

Serves 6–8

Put the cream, lemon rind and sugar in a saucepan. Stir over a gentle heat for about 10 minutes until the sugar has completely dissolved, bringing just to the boil. Cool, stirring from time to time, and when almost cold add strained lemon juice. Crumble macaroons and put in the bottom of an attractive glass bowl. Pour the cold cream mixture over the macaroons. Chill overnight in the refrigerator.

Serve chilled and decorated with lemon zest.

AN EXCELLENT LEMON PUDDING

This lovely pudding is based on a very old recipe, which was baked in a dish lined with puff pastry. By whisking egg whites and adding just before baking, the pudding will be very light. You may need to cover it with greaseproof paper if the top is getting brown too quickly before the underneath has set. This pudding separates out during cooking into a tangy custard layer with a featherlight sponge topping. An orange or lime version of the pudding can be made in the same way.

100g (3½oz) butter, softened
175g (6oz) caster sugar
Grated rind and juice of
    4 lemons
4 eggs, separated
125ml (4fl oz) full-cream milk
50g (1¾oz) plain flour

Serves 4–6

Cream the butter and sugar together until white and fluffy, then beat in the lemon rind and juice. Beat the egg yolks into the creamed mixture very gradually. When the mixture is very light, beat in the milk. Fold in the sieved flour.

Whisk the egg whites until they are firm and stand in peaks. Fold them gently into the lemon mixture, then pour into a buttered 20cm (8in) soufflé dish. Place the dish in a roasting tin and pour hot water into the tin until it comes halfway up the sides of the dish.

Bake in the centre of a preheated oven at 180°C, 350°F, gas mark 4, for about 45 minutes, until the top is golden brown and the pudding has risen.

Serve warm, or cold with cream.

MOONSHINE

This romantically named pudding is a lemony jelly, popular with 17th- and 18th-century cooks. Saffron would probably have been used to colour the jelly in the 17th century as highly coloured foods were extremely popular. Make it in a fancy Victorian mould if you have one.

115g (4oz) caster sugar
Finely pared rind of 2 lemons
600ml (1 pint) cold water
Juice of 2 lemons, strained
15g (½oz) gelatine

Serves 4–6

Put the sugar, lemon rind and water in a saucepan. Bring to the boil and simmer for 15 minutes to allow the lemon rind to infuse. Leave on one side to cool. Strain. Put the strained lemon juice in a cup and sprinkle the gelatine over the top. Place the cup in a pan of water and gently heat until the gelatine has melted. Strain through a warmed fine-mesh sieve into the cooled lemon syrup. Stir well to make sure the gelatine is mixed in thoroughly. Leave to cool again and, when just beginning to set, whisk until the jelly looks like snow. Turn into a wetted mould and refrigerate until set.

Turn out on to an attractive plate by dipping the mould quickly in hot water. Serve chilled and decorated with a few small edible flowers and maidenhair fern, if you have a plant. Eat with homemade dessert biscuits.

CHERRIES IN RED WINE

Cherries became very popular in Britain towards the end of the Middle Ages, although the Romans had cultivated them much earlier and they were very common in monastery gardens. They are often mentioned in folklore and have been linked to the cuckoo, which reputedly stops singing only after it has eaten three good meals of cherries.

900g (2lb) dark red cherries
25g (1oz) sugar
Pinch of ground cinnamon
150ml (¼ pint) red wine
3 tablespoons redcurrant jelly
Juice of 1 orange
1–1½ dessertspoons arrowroot
1–2 tablespoons cold water
3–4 sugar lumps
1 orange
300ml (½ pint) double cream
Orange rind and cherries
     to decorate

Serves 6

Stone the cherries and place in a saucepan with the sugar and cinnamon. Cover the pan and heat gently until the juices run freely, about 7–10 minutes. By this time the cherries will be at boiling point. Remove from the heat, drain the cherries and turn into a serving bowl, reserving the juice. Put the wine in the saucepan and boil rapidly until reduced by half. Add the redcurrant jelly and orange juice and heat gently until the jelly has melted. Add the juice from the cherries. Dissolve 1 dessertspoon of arrowroot in 1 tablespoon of water and add this to the saucepan. Bring to boiling point again. The liquor should now be smooth and rich-looking but not gluey. You may need more arrowroot – it really depends on the juiciness of your cherries. Pour the juice over the cherries and chill well.

Rub sugar lumps over the rind of the orange until they are orange-coloured and well impregnated. Crush them in a bowl and add the strained juice of the orange. Whip the cream lightly, until it will barely hold its shape. Fold in the orange syrup. Chill well. Serve separately or pour over the top of the cherries in their serving bowl. Decorate with orange rind and whole cherries.

PLUMS IN SLOE GIN

Large Victoria plums have the best flavour for this dish, so make the most of them when they are in season, around late August.

900g (2lb) firm, but ripe, plums
115g (4oz) soft brown sugar
1 teaspoon vanilla extract
200ml (7fl oz) sloe gin,
     homemade or bought

Serves 4–6

Preheat the oven to 180°C, 350°F, gas mark 4. Halve and stone the plums, then place them in one layer in a large shallow ovenproof dish. Sprinkle with the sugar.

Stir the vanilla extract into the sloe gin and pour over the plums. Cover tightly with foil and place in the oven for about 45 minutes. Baste the plums once during this time, taking care not to break them up. The plums should be cooked, but not falling apart, and sitting in a puddle of gloriously boozy crimson syrup.

Serve the plums barely warm, or at room temperature, with their juices and some thick cream.

APRICOT AMBER PUDDING

Traditionally, an Amber Pudding was made with apples and baked in a puff-pastry case. It is a very old-fashioned sweet dating back to the 18th century, and can be made with many other fruits such as apples, rhubarb, gooseberries, blackberries, blackcurrants or plums.

175g (6oz) shortcrust pastry
   (see page 10)
450g (1lb) fresh apricots
About 150g (5½oz) caster sugar
1 teaspoon lemon juice
25g (1oz) unsalted butter
2 eggs, separated
Pinch of salt
Crystallized apricot and angelica
   to decorate

Serves 6

Preheat the oven to 200°C, 400°F, gas mark 6, with a large baking sheet in the oven to warm up as well. Roll out the pastry thinly and use to line a buttered 20cm (8in) shallow ovenproof dish. Chill in the refrigerator for 30 minutes. Prick the base and line with baking paper and baking beans. Place in the oven on the hot baking sheet and bake blind for about 10 minutes, then remove the baking parchment and beans and cook for about another 10 minutes to dry out the inside without browning the pastry.

Meanwhile, wash and stone the apricots, then poach in a little water until tender. Rub the fruit through a plastic sieve, then sweeten with sugar to taste (about 30g (1½oz)), adding the lemon juice. Stir in the butter and beat in the egg yolks. Leave on one side to cool.

Pour the cooled apricot mixture into the cooked pastry case and cook for 20 minutes in the preheated oven.

Whisk the egg whites with the salt until stiff, but not dry. Add 60g (2oz) caster sugar and whisk until stiff again. Fold in another 60g (2oz) sugar gently. Reduce the oven temperature to 180°C, 350°F, gas mark 4. Pile the meringue on top of the apricot mixture and spread out, making sure that it touches the edges of the pastry. Dust with extra caster sugar and bake in the centre of the oven for 20 minutes, or until the meringue is crisp and very lightly browned.

Serve warm or cold with whipped cream and decorated with pieces of crystallized apricot and candied angelica, if you wish.

RHUBARB AND ORANGE FOOL

Rhubarb was one of the last garden fruits to be cultivated for eating in Britain. It first arrived in the 17th century, its cultivation spread rapidly throughout Britain and it has remained one of the most popular garden fruits. An old-fashioned rhubarb or spring fool is the perfect way to round off a spring dinner party, especially if the meal has been rather rich. Young forced rhubarb makes the best fool, because of its beautiful pink colour when cooked.

900g (2lb) rhubarb
Grated rind of 1 orange
½ teaspoon ground ginger
5cm (2in) stick cinnamon
25g (1oz) unsalted butter
About 175g (6oz) caster sugar
600ml (1 pint) double or
   whipping cream
2 tablespoons orange liqueur
   (optional)
Primroses or other edible spring
   flowers to decorate

Serves 8–10

Cut the rhubarb into short lengths. Put in a large saucepan with orange rind, ginger, cinnamon stick, butter and sugar. Cook over a gentle heat for about five minutes until the rhubarb is softened, thick and pulpy. Remove the cinnamon stick and cool completely.

Whip the cream with the liqueur, if using, until thick enough to hold its shape. Fold in the cold rhubarb pulp very lightly to give a marbled effect. Taste, and add more sugar if necessary. Spoon the fool into a deep glass bowl or individual glasses, and chill well before serving. Decorate with primroses, or other simple edible spring flowers.

Right: Rhubarb and Orange Fool
Next page: Apricot Amber Pudding

RHUBARB AND RED WINE JELLY

An ideal pudding after a rich meal. Use young, pink, forced rhubarb for the best colour and flavour. Make in a traditional-style jelly mould, if possible.

450g (1lb) young or forced rhubarb
5cm (2in) piece of fresh ginger
150g (5½oz) cane sugar
Juice of 2 lemons
Juice of 2 oranges
850ml (1½ pints) red wine
4 tablespoons water
40g (1½oz) gelatine
Primroses or other edible spring flowers to decorate

Serves 6–8

Cut the rhubarb into 2.5cm (1in) pieces and place in a large pan with the peeled and roughly chopped ginger. Add the sugar and strain the lemon and orange juices into the mixture through a fine sieve, then add the wine.

Set the pan over the heat, bring to the boil, then simmer gently for about 15 minutes, or until the rhubarb is completely mushy. Remove the pan from the heat and strain the liquid through the finest sieve into another bowl or a clean pan. Don't press the rhubarb against the sieve, or the juices will become cloudy.

Put the 4 tablespoons of water into a small pan, bring to bubbling point and remove from the heat. Sprinkle the gelatine over the top and stir until completely dissolved. Pass through a sieve into the rhubarb and wine liquor, then pour into a 1.3 litre (2¼ pint) jelly mould. Leave until cold, then transfer to the refrigerator to set.

Just before serving, dip the mould in hot water for a few seconds, then turn the jelly out on to a cake stand or serving plate, giving it a good shake to release it. Decorate with primroses or other edible spring flowers and serve with cream.

Left: Rhubarb and Red Wine Jelly
Previous page: Cranachan

CRANACHAN

A traditional Scottish pudding which started life as a hot drink similar to the Elizabethan version of syllabub and was later thickened with oatmeal. Fragrant heather honey, Scotch whisky and Scottish raspberries are traditional, but other fruits and alcohol can be used.

85g (3oz) coarse oatmeal
300ml (½ pint) double cream
50g (1¾oz) caster sugar
50ml (2fl oz) malt whisky
350g (12oz) fresh raspberries,
    reserving a few for
    decoration
Sprigs of fresh mint

Serves 4–6

Sprinkle the oatmeal on to a baking tray. Bake in a preheated oven at 200°C, 400°F, gas mark 6, until browned and crisp, moving the oatmeal around to prevent sticking and burning. Remove from the oven and cool.

Whip the cream with the sugar and whisky until it stands in fairly soft peaks. Gently fold in the cooled toasted oatmeal. Spoon into individual glasses, layering the raspberries between spoonfuls of the mixture as you go. Serve decorated with a few raspberries and a sprig of fresh mint.

VARIATION

CRANACHAN WITH STRAWBERRIES

Quarter 600g (1lb 5oz) strawberries and leave to soak in 25g (1oz) caster sugar and 50ml (2fl oz) raspberry liqueur for at least 10 minutes. Gently heat the oatmeal and 50g (1¾oz) soft brown sugar for 2–3 minutes, stirring continuously until the sugar has dissolved and the oatmeal is golden and caramelized. Remove from the heat and spread the oatmeal on a plate to cool, breaking up any large clusters with a fork. Continue as before.

PORT WINE JELLY

This posh jelly makes a very good alternative to plum pudding for Christmas lunch.

300ml (½ pint) cold water
115g (4oz) cane sugar, preferably cubes
1 tablespoon redcurrant jelly
2.5cm (1in) piece of cinnamon stick
3 cloves
1 bay leaf
Grated rind of 1 lemon
1 blade of mace
300ml (½ pint) ruby port
1 tablespoon brandy
15g (½oz) gelatine

Serves 6

Place the cold water, sugar, redcurrant jelly, cinnamon stick, cloves, bay leaf, lemon rind and mace in a clean saucepan over a gentle heat, stirring occasionally. When the sugar has completely dissolved and the jelly has melted, bring to the boil. Simmer for 10 minutes.

Put the port and brandy into a second clean saucepan and heat gently. Sprinkle on the gelatine and bring to the boil. Simmer for 10 minutes. Strain the contents of both saucepans through a fine sieve into a large jug, stir, and as the jelly cools pour into 6 stemmed glass dishes. Leave to set in the refrigerator.

Serve chilled with pouring cream and homemade shortbread.

DAMSON SNOW

This also makes a super ice cream. Freeze in the normal way.

900g (2lb) damsons
175g (6oz) caster sugar
90ml (3fl oz) cold water
425ml (¾ pint) double cream
2 tablespoons brandy or Marsala
    (optional)
3 egg whites

Serves 6

Put washed and de-stalked damsons into a saucepan with sugar and water. Bring slowly to the boil and cook gently for 10–15 minutes or until the fruit is tender. Rub through a sieve and leave the damson pulp to get cold.

Lightly whip the cream with brandy or Marsala, if using, until thick. Whisk the egg whites until stiff and fold into the cream mixture. Stir in the damson pulp, reserving 1 tablespoon for decoration. Pour into individual glasses and chill well. Just before serving, stir in the reserved damson pulp to give a marbled effect, or just top with damson pulp. Serve with homemade dessert biscuits.

EDINBURGH FOG

This delicious Scottish variation of Damson Snow leaves out the damsons and adds ratafia biscuits.

ADDITIONAL INGREDIENTS:

2 tablespoons sweet sherry
　　or Madeira
55g (2oz) ratafia biscuits
Caster sugar to taste
Toasted flaked almonds
Fresh raspberries or
　　strawberries

Serves 6

Omit the damsons. Whip the cream with 2 tablespoons of sweet sherry or Madeira. Stir in the ratafia biscuits and sweeten to taste with caster sugar. Chill well, then sprinkle generously with toasted flaked almonds. Serve with fresh raspberries or strawberries.

SUMMER PUDDING

The true old-fashioned Summer Pudding was made with raspberries and redcurrants only, but if you wish, you can include small halved strawberries, white currants, blueberries, sweet, firm-fleshed cherries and a few blackcurrants – not many of the latter or they will dominate the pudding. If you are lucky enough to be able to get hold of some mulberries, they make a delicious summer pudding, combined with half the amount of strawberries. Make sure you use good-quality bread.

700g (1lb 9oz) fresh raspberries
200g (7oz) fresh redcurrants
115g (4oz) vanilla caster sugar
   or plain caster sugar
About 6 slices of day-old white
   bread about 8mm (⅜in) thick
2 tablespoons raspberry liqueur

Serves 6

Put the fruit into a heavy saucepan and sprinkle over the sugar. Heat gently for 3–4 minutes only, until the sugar has dissolved and the juices have begun to flow. Cut the crusts off the bread and use it to line an 850ml (1½ pint) pudding basin, bottom and sides. Overlap the slices slightly so that there are no gaps. Spoon the fruit into the basin, reserving a little of the juice for serving. Pour the raspberry liqueur over the fruit before finishing with a top layer of bread.

Put a plate on top that fits exactly inside the basin and weight it fairly heavily. Leave the pudding in the refrigerator overnight. Turn out just before serving and pour the reserved juice over any bread that isn't quite soaked through. Serve chilled with pouring cream or softly whipped double cream.

SPICED WINTER PUDDING

This delicious variation of Summer Pudding makes a great spicy dish for winter, although it is served cold.

175g (6oz) dried apricots
350g (12oz) peeled, cored and
   sliced cooking apples
50g (1¾oz) raisins
1 level teaspoon ground
   cinnamon
2 tablespoons warm water
15g (½oz) gelatine
115–175g (4–6oz) caster sugar
   (to taste)
About 6 slices of day-old white
   bread about 8mm (⅜in) thick
Whipped cream and raisins to
   decorate

Soak the dried apricots in 600ml (1 pint) water overnight. Place the apricots and soaking liquor in a saucepan and bring to boil. Simmer uncovered for 10–15 minutes. Strain the apricots, reserving the liquor. Return 300ml (½ pint) of liquor to the saucepan with the peeled, cored and sliced cooking apples, the raisins and the ground cinnamon. Cook until the apples are soft. Add the apricots. Put 2 tablespoons of warm water in a cup and sprinkle on the gelatine. Place the cup in a small saucepan of hot water and heat gently to dissolve the agent. Pour through a warmed fine-mesh sieve into the fruit mixture (this ensures that any tiny lumps are removed. If the sieve is not warm, a thin layer of gelatine will remain on it and then your proportions will be wrong). Add the caster sugar to taste and leave to cool a little. Line and fill the basin as described for the Summer Pudding. Just before serving, unmould the pudding and decorate with whipped cream and raisins. Serve very cold.

CLARE COLLEGE MUSH

Also called Eton Mess, the original recipe for this traditional pudding is said to have come from Clare College, Cambridge. A delicious combination of strawberries, cream and crushed meringues, it can be flavoured with an orange or berry liqueur or vanilla. Other fruits work well – raspberries and poached apricots, rhubarb, damsons and plums are favourites, but best of all I like a combination of strawberries and raspberries with a flavouring of liqueur and half cream and half yoghurt.

2 large egg whites
50g (2oz) caster sugar
50g (2oz) icing sugar
225g (8oz) fresh strawberries
225g (8oz) fresh raspberries
1 tablespoon (plus an extra
    dash) raspberry liqueur
200ml (7fl oz) double cream
200ml (7fl oz) natural yoghurt

Serves 6

Preheat the oven to 100°C, 200°F, gas mark ¼. Whisk the egg whites until they form soft peaks, then beat in the caster sugar a little at a time. Continue whisking for a further 10 minutes until the mix is smooth and shiny, then sift in the icing sugar. Spoon on to non-stick baking paper arranged on a baking tray to make individual meringues, then bake in the oven until dry, but with a slightly soft, chewy centre – this should take about 2 hours. Remove from the oven and leave to cool on a wire rack.

When ready to assemble the pudding – and it is best eaten within 2 hours of making – cut the strawberries into halves or quarters, depending on their size, then toss with a dash of raspberry liqueur. Stir in the raspberries, reserving a few of the best for decoration.

Lightly whip the cream and yoghurt with a tablespoon of raspberry liqueur. Break the meringues into walnut-sized pieces and gently stir into the cream mixture with the fruit (don't overmix, because it looks best with a raspberry-ripple effect).

Spoon into glass dishes and serve chilled, decorated with the reserved raspberries.

Right: Clare College Mush

APPLE AND BRANDY TRIFLE

A popular Victorian recipe from Mrs Beeton. The slightly acidic poached apples counteract the richness of the custard and cream topping.

1 fatless sponge made with
   3 eggs, 85g (3oz) caster sugar
   and 85g (3oz) plain flour
About 6 tablespoons apple brandy
3 large Bramley apples
3 Cox's apples
2 tablespoons soft brown sugar
½ teaspoon ground cinnamon
725ml (1¼ pint) double cream
1 vanilla pod, split lengthways
2 large eggs
2 large egg yolks
85g (3oz) caster sugar
25g (1oz) icing sugar
Vanilla extract to taste
100g (3½oz) flaked almonds
25g (1oz) icing sugar
3 tablespoons apple brandy

Serves 6–8

Cut the sponge into 2.5cm (1in) slices and arrange in a large bowl. Pour over the apple brandy and leave for at least 30 minutes to soak in. To make the apple layer, peel, core and roughly chop the apples. Place in a saucepan with the sugar and cinnamon. Cook over a medium heat until the apples are tender, then set aside to cool.

To make the custard, pour 425ml (¾ pint) double cream into a saucepan with the vanilla pod and bring to the boil. Meanwhile, mix the eggs, egg yolks and sugar together in a large bowl. When the cream reaches boiling point, pour it over the egg mixture, whisking continuously to prevent the eggs from curdling. Strain through a fine sieve into a large bowl. Place over a pan of simmering water. Heat until the custard has thickened, whisking from time to time. Set aside to cool. Cover the soaked sponge with a layer of the cooked apple mixture, then a layer of custard.

For the cream topping, whisk together the remaining cream, icing sugar and vanilla until soft peaks are formed. Spoon on top of the custard layer.

Mix the almonds, icing sugar and apple brandy together in a small bowl. Tip out on to a baking tray and toast in a preheated oven at 180°C, 350°F, gas mark 4 for 15 minutes, or until golden brown. Leave to cool, then scatter over the cream to decorate.

Left: Apple and Brandy Trifle

MOTHER EVE'S PUDDING

Traditionally made with tempting apples under a sponge topping, hence the name! However, you can use any fruit and the flavourings can be varied accordingly by adding spices or orange rind. The Georgian recipe for this pudding was made with suet and included currants as well as the apples. It was also boiled rather than baked.

600g (1lb 5oz) cooking apples
85g (3oz) caster sugar
Grated rind of 1 lemon
2 cloves
1 tablespoon water
115g (4oz) salted butter
115g (4oz) caster sugar
2 eggs
¼ teaspoon vanilla extract
115g (4oz) self-raising flour
1 tablespoon warm water
Caster sugar for dusting

Serves 6

Butter a 1.2 litre (2 pint) ovenproof dish. Peel, core and slice the apples thinly and place in a heavy saucepan with the sugar, lemon rind, cloves and water. Heat over a gentle heat for a few minutes until just tender. Turn into the prepared dish and leave to cool.

Cream butter and sugar together in a mixing bowl until pale and fluffy. Beat the eggs and add gradually to the creamed mixture, beating well after each addition. Beat in the vanilla essence, and gently fold the sieved flour into the creamed mixture. Stir in the warm water to make a soft dropping consistency and spread evenly over the apples.

Bake in the centre of a preheated oven at 190°C, 375°F, gas mark 5 for about 45 minutes, or until well risen and golden brown (test with a fine skewer, which should come out clean). Serve hot or cold, dusted with caster sugar and with Vanilla Custard Sauce or Lemon Sauce (see pages 95 and 92).

APPLE AND ALMOND PUDDING

This is a delicious variation on Mother Eve's Pudding.

ALTERNATIVE INGREDIENT:
115g (4oz) ground almonds

Prepare the pudding as instructed opposite but substitute the self-raising flour with ground almonds. Continue as before. Serve hot or cold with pouring cream.

APPLE AND MARMALADE PUDDING

This further variation uses marmalade to give an orangey flavour.

ADDITIONAL INGREDIENT:
2 rounded tablespoons Seville orange marmalade

Make as before, but stir 2 rounded tablespoons Seville orange marmalade into the apple mixture, reducing the sugar to just 25g (1oz) or less.

VICTORIAN APPLE SNOW

This dish of apples and whisked egg whites has ancient ancestors. Egg whites were first beaten in Elizabethan days and used to produce their 'dishful of snow', a spectacular centrepiece for the banquet course following a festive meal. They were beaten with thick cream, rose-water and sugar until the froth rose and was gathered in a colander. This was built up over an apple and a bed of rosemary on a platter.

1kg (2lb 4oz) Bramley apples

1 tablespoon lemon juice

3 tablespoons sweet cider or water

Grated rind of 1 lemon

About 85g (3oz) caster sugar

Pinch of ground cinnamon (optional)

3 egg whites

About 4 teaspoons golden muscovado sugar, to decorate

Edible fresh flowers, to decorate

Serves 6

Peel, core and thinly slice the apples. Put in a heavy saucepan with the lemon juice, cider or water, and lemon rind. Cover and cook over a very low heat until quite soft and fluffy, stirring once or twice. Then remove the lid and continue cooking, stirring frequently, until the apples are reduced to a foam and most of the moisture has been driven off. Remove from the heat and stir in sugar to taste – remember that half the charm of this traditional dish is its light, fruity freshness, so it should be quite tart. Stir in cinnamon if using, then beat until smooth with a wooden spoon. Turn into a dish and leave to become cold.

Whisk egg whites until they stand in shiny peaks. Lightly fold in the cold apple purée and spoon into individual glasses. Refrigerate.

Immediately before serving, sprinkle with muscovado sugar and decorate with edible fresh flowers. Daisies look particularly lovely with this simple pudding. Eat with little dessert biscuits, homemade if possible.

BLACK CAPS

Apples were first baked in the ashes of the fire. The skins were often burnt on one side, hence the name Black Caps. Baked apples, frequently cooked in cider or wine, have continued to be a country favourite for centuries. They can be filled with any dried fruit and are delicious topped with honey, jam or marmalade. The secret of a good baked apple is to use a quality cooking apple, preferably a Bramley. This large apple with a shiny green skin is very crisp and cooks superbly.

6 large Bramley cooking apples
50g (1¾oz) chopped dates
50g (1¾oz) sultanas
50g (1¾oz) raisins
25g (1oz) chopped almonds
    or hazelnuts
Grated rind and juice of
    1 orange
85g (3oz) soft brown sugar
1 level teaspoon ground mace
    or mixed spice
40g (1½oz) butter
150ml (¼ pint) sweet sherry
    or Madeira

Serves 6

Wash and core the apples. Score the skin around the middle of each apple to prevent it bursting during baking, and stand close together in a well-buttered ovenproof dish. Mix chopped dates, sultanas, raisins and chopped nuts with the orange rind and juice. Pack the centres of the apples with this mixture. Mix brown sugar and spice together and sprinkle over each apple. Top with a knob of butter. Pour sherry or Madeira around the apples and bake in the centre of a preheated oven at 180°C, 350°F, gas mark 4 for 45–60 minutes, basting occasionally. Serve warm, topped with thick cream and/or Stem Ginger Ice Cream or Honey and Brandy Ice Cream (see pages 71 and 72) and extra brown sugar.

VARIATION

ICED APPLES

Prepare as for Black Caps, but remove the apples from the oven about 15 minutes before the end of the cooking time. Strip off the top half of the skin. Whisk 2 or 3 egg whites very stiffly and add 60–85g (2¼–3oz) caster sugar. Whisk again until stiff and glossy and then gently fold in another 60–85g (2¼–3oz) caster sugar. Coat the baked apples with this meringue and return to the oven for a further 15 minutes, until the meringue is crisp and lightly browned.

SPICED PEARS IN RED WINE

The earliest pears were called 'wardens' and were extremely hard. Many recipes like this were devised for cooking them slowly for several hours until they softened. Cider, or sweet white wine, can replace the red wine, if desired.

4 large, good-shaped hard pears
   with stalks
300ml (½ pint) red wine
85g (3oz) caster sugar
1 vanilla pod, split in half
   lengthways
1 small cinnamon stick
4 cloves
Zest of 1 orange
1 thick slice of fresh ginger,
   peeled
1 rounded teaspoon arrowroot

Serves 4

Preheat the oven to 130°C, 250°F, gas mark ½. Peel the pears thinly with a potato peeler, leaving the stalks intact. Remove the 'eyes' opposite the stalk ends and cut a thin slice from the bottom of each pear so that they stand upright easily. Lay the pears on their side in a flameproof casserole dish with a tight-fitting lid.

Pour over the wine and sprinkle over the sugar. Scrape the seeds out of the vanilla pod and add to the casserole with the pod, cinnamon stick, cloves, orange zest and ginger.

Bring everything up to simmering point, then cover the casserole and bake on a low shelf in the oven for about 1½ hours. Turn the pears on to their other side and cook for a further 1½ hours. When the pears are cooked, carefully lift them out with a slotted spoon, standing them upright in a dish.

Strain the cooking liquor into a bowl, then pour back into the casserole. Place over a direct heat. Mix the arrowroot to a smooth paste with a little cold water, then add to the wine mixture, whisking all the time. Bring just up to simmering point, when the liquor will have thickened. Remove from the heat and cool.

Spoon over the pears when cool and baste well. Cover the dish with foil and chill thoroughly in the refrigerator, basting frequently with the wine sauce. Serve bathed in the sauce, with Vanilla Ice Cream (see page 74) or thick cream.

GOOSEBERRY AND ELDERFLOWER FOOL

'Soft, pale, creamy, untroubled, the English fruit fool is the most frail and insubstantial of English summer dishes',
wrote Elizabeth David. The fruit fool, probably named after the French verb fouler, meaning 'to crush', is one of the
few quintessentially English puddings that should not be tampered with – for me, the perfect fool is just cream,
fruit (flavoured or plain) and sugar.

450g (1lb) green gooseberries
3 or 4 large elderflower heads in
    full bloom
1 tablespoon water
85–115g (3–4oz) caster sugar
300ml (½ pint) double cream

Serves 4–6

Wash and top and tail the gooseberries. Put in a heavy saucepan with the elderflower heads tied together with cotton thread, the water and the sugar. Cook gently until the fruit is soft, then set aside to cool. Once cool, lift out the elderflower stalks – don't worry about leaving the flowers behind, they will add to the flavour.

Mash the gooseberries with a fork and taste for sweetness (if you prefer a smoother purée, rub the gooseberries through a plastic sieve). Leave to get completely cold.

Whip the double cream until thick and just beginning to hold its shape. Fold into the gooseberry purée to give a swirled, marbled effect, then pile into a serving bowl or individual glasses. Decorate with small sprigs of elderflower, if in season. Ideally, serve with homemade biscuits.

VARIATIONS

Any fruits can be used to make fools, but for me, the most successful are berries, currants, apricots, the plum family and of course, rhubarb.

MRS BEETON'S GOOSEBERRY TRIFLE

In this recipe, gooseberry pulp has replaced the more usual sponge cake at the bottom of the trifle, and is covered with a rich custard and topped with a 'whip', which was a Victorian version of syllabub. If possible, make the syllabub topping a day in advance. Any fruit pulp can be used.

Grated rind and juice of
   1 lemon
6 tablespoons sweet white wine
   or sherry
2 tablespoons brandy
50g (1¾oz) caster sugar
600ml (1 pint) double cream
700g (1lb 9oz) green
   gooseberries
3 tablespoons cold water
250g (9oz) caster sugar
Strip of lemon peel
4 egg yolks
1 level teaspoon cornflour
Lemon peel and sprigs of
   rosemary to garnish

Serves 6

Put the lemon rind and juice into a small bowl. Stir in the wine or sherry, brandy and sugar until the sugar has dissolved. Cover and leave for several hours to infuse. Strain the liquid into a clean bowl and stir in 300ml (½ pint) of the cream gradually, beating until it almost reaches a soft peak stage (don't use an electric beater; if overbeaten, the syllabub will become grainy). Chill overnight.

Next day, top and tail the gooseberries and put in a heavy saucepan with the water and 50g (1¾oz) sugar. Simmer gently for about 20 minutes until soft. Rub through a sieve or beat to a pulp. Add 175g (6oz) sugar – you may need more if the gooseberries are tart. Put in a shallow serving bowl and leave to cool.

Bring the remaining 300ml (½ pint) of cream slowly to the boil with the lemon peel, and leave on one side to cool a little. Cream the egg yolks, cornflour and 25g (1oz) caster sugar together until almost white. Remove the lemon rind and pour on the hot cream in a steady stream, beating all the time. Rinse out the saucepan used for heating the cream, leaving a film of water in the bottom. Return the egg mixture to the pan and heat gently until thick enough to coat the back of a wooden spoon (don't boil because the custard will curdle). Remove from the heat and leave to cool. Pour over the gooseberry pulp. Sprinkle with caster sugar to stop a skin forming and leave to get completely cold.

Pile the syllabub on top of the custard and chill. Just before serving, decorate with twists of lemon peel and sprigs of rosemary.

GOOSEBERRY TANSY

This very old pudding was so called from the use of the herb tansy. It was chopped up with the fruit, but is seldom used in cookery today as it has rather a bitter flavour. Apples, rhubarb or plums can be used instead of gooseberries.

450g (1lb) green gooseberries
115g (4oz) unsalted butter
2 egg yolks
150ml (¼ pint) double cream
About 2 tablespoons
    caster sugar
Juice of ½ lemon

Serves 4

Simmer the gooseberries in the butter until cooked – about 15 minutes. Remove from the heat and cool a little. Stir in the beaten egg yolks and lightly whipped cream. Sweeten with sugar to taste. Bring to the boil very gently and when thick, turn into a china serving bowl. Sprinkle with caster sugar and lemon juice. Serve cold.

BRANDIED PEACHES

Peaches were introduced by the Romans and by the 17th century there were 22 varieties growing in Britain. Recipes for brandied fruit, one of the early ways of preserving, began to appear at the beginning of the 18th century. Peaches, nectarines, apricots, cherries and grapes were packed into earthenware jars containing brandy and a little sugar syrup. The jars were sealed closely and the fruit was stored for future use.

6 fresh peaches
Boiling water to cover peaches
Juice of 1 lemon
12 cloves
300ml (½ pint) cold water
115g (4oz) granulated sugar
5cm (2in) piece of cinnamon
    stick
1 bay leaf
25g (1oz) butter
2 tablespoons brandy

Serves 6

Cover the peaches with boiling water for about 2 minutes. Remove from the water, and skin. Halve and stone the peaches. Brush all over with lemon juice to stop them discolouring. Stick a clove in each half. Put the water, sugar, cinnamon stick, bay leaf and butter into a small saucepan. Bring slowly to the boil to dissolve the sugar. When it has completely dissolved, boil for 5 minutes to make a sugar syrup. Place the peaches in a shallow ovenproof dish. Add brandy to the sugar syrup and pour over the peaches. Cover and bake in the centre of a preheated oven at 160°C, 325°F, gas mark 3 for about 30 minutes, or until the peaches are tender, but still hold their shape. Remove the bay leaf and cinnamon stick and serve either hot or cold with whipped cream.

NECTARINES BAKED IN CREAM

This delicious fruit has been known in Britain since the early 17th century and was frequently grown in the walled gardens of great houses. Peaches, pears and apricots are equally good in this recipe.

6 fresh nectarines
300ml (½ pint) double cream
115g (4oz) caster sugar
1 vanilla pod, split in half
    lengthways
25g (1oz) toasted flaked
    almonds

Serves 6

Skin the nectarines by dropping them in boiling water for a few minutes. Remove the stones by running a knife round the fruit and twisting the two halves in opposite directions. Place the nectarine halves in a shallow ovenproof dish. Heat the cream, sugar and vanilla pod together gently until the sugar has dissolved. Pour the cream over the nectarines (don't remove the vanilla pod). Bake in the centre of a moderate oven at 180°C, 350°F, gas mark 4 for 30–40 minutes or until the fruit is tender. Remove from the oven and chill well.

Serve very cold, sprinkled with toasted flaked almonds. This dish is also very good served with hot Easy Chocolate Sauce (see page 67) dribbled over the cream.

VARIATION

CREAMY NECTARINE TART

Line a 30cm (12in) flan tin with shortcrust pastry. Bake blind for 10–15 minutes at 200°C, 400°F, gas mark 6 (see Apricot Amber Pudding, page 23, for instructions on baking blind). Fill the cooked pastry case with the nectarine and cream mixture as above and bake for a further 30 minutes.

CREAMY PUDDINGS

England's elaborate and elegant cold sweets were famous throughout Europe in Tudor times. The sweet course at a great feast was then known as the 'banquet' and consisted of preserved fruits, creams, flummeries, jellies, fools and tarts. Some noblemen built banqueting houses in their grounds to serve the banquet privately to their guests after the main part of the meal had been eaten in the Great Hall. On prosperous farms these dishes were less elaborately served and decorated, but the same cold sweets, rich with cream, butter, eggs and fruit, were made for special occasions.

The ancestor of creams, fools and flummeries was the medieval meatless pottage known as 'frumenty', made from breadcrumbs, oats, rice, wheat or barley, stewed in almond milk and served on fasting days. Cream later replaced the milk and almonds were used for thickening. This dish was known as 'whitepot'. By the 17th century, the almonds were often omitted and the cream was thickened with eggs. Sometimes fresh or boiled cream was sweetened and mixed with fruit pulp to make fruit fools or creams.

In the 18th century, gooseberries and orange juice combined with eggs were made into fools, and recipes for almond and codlin or apple cream were very common. These fruit creams were served in the second course alongside flummeries and jellies. Iced creams and snows were also being made at this time.

The syllabub of Tudor and Stuart times was designed to be drunk and consisted of white wine, cider or fruit juice, sugar and nutmeg, to which cream or milk was whisked. The object was to produce a frothy head to the drink with a clear liquid below. The latter was drunk from the spout of a 'syllabub pot', while the creamy foam was eaten. In Georgian times the cream and wine were whisked together with lemon juice – these whipped-cream syllabubs remained a very popular dessert all through the 18th century and have become fashionable again in the last few years.

There are so many delicious recipes for these creamy puddings that it has been impossible to include even a reasonable number in this chapter, but I hope you will enjoy those I have mentioned and that they will inspire you to experiment with other favourite fruits and flavourings yourselves.

ELDERFLOWER TRIFLE

Elderflowers were used widely in the past to flavour jellies, creams, flummeries, fools and trifles. Pick them on a dry day. This trifle has a base of Amaretti or ratafia biscuits, with a creamy syllabub topping. It looks prettiest in individual stemmed glasses.

FOR THE SYLLABUB
Grated rind and juice of
   1 large lemon
125ml (4fl oz) white wine
1 large elderflower head
   in full bloom
85g (3oz) caster sugar
Pinch of freshly grated nutmeg
300ml (½ pint) double cream
Sprigs of elderflower to
   decorate

FOR THE BASE
8 Amaretti biscuits
2 tablespoons homemade or
   good-quality elderflower
   cordial
2 tablespoons sweet sherry
2 tablespoons cold water

Serves 4

Begin by making the liquid base for the syllabub. Mix together the lemon rind, juice, wine and flowers snipped from the elderflower head. Set aside to steep for at least 1 hour.

Meanwhile, put the biscuits, broken, into 4 glasses. Mix the cordial, sherry and water together and pour equal amounts into each glass.

Strain the steeped syllabub liquid into a large bowl. Stir in the sugar and the nutmeg, then pour in the cream. Whisk together until the cream thickens, then spoon into the glasses.

Serve chilled and decorated with a few tiny sprigs of elderflower, either fresh or crystallized. Elderflower can be crystallized by dipping it into beaten egg white, then into sugar and leaving it on a wire rack to dry.

LEMON POSSET

A posset was an Elizabethan drink made of milk curdled with sack (sack is the old name of a Spanish wine similar to sherry) or claret, beer, ale and orange or lemon juice – rather like a syllabub. Breadcrumbs were added to thicken the posset so that it could be eaten rather than drunk. Later, these were omitted and beaten egg whites were used instead to make it lighter and not so rich.

600ml (1 pint) double or
   whipping cream
Grated rind of 1½ lemons
150ml (¼ pint) dry white wine
4 tablespoons lemon juice
About 115g (4oz) caster sugar
3 large egg whites
2 tablespoons caster sugar
Extra lemon zest for decorating

Serves 6

Beat the cream and lemon rind in a mixing bowl until thick. Beat in the wine until thick again. Add the lemon juice very gradually, beating all the time. Add sugar to taste and beat until stiff. Whisk the egg whites until stiff and standing in peaks, then whisk in the 2 tablespoons of sugar until smooth and glossy. Fold the egg whites into the cream mixture, then pile into a glass or china bowl. Serve chilled and decorated with lemon zest. Accompany with homemade dessert biscuits.

VARIATION
ORANGE POSSET
Substitute grated rind of 1 orange for 1 lemon and 2 tablespoons orange juice for 2 tablespoons of the lemon juice. Decorate with orange zest.

WHIM-WHAM

This Edwardian trifle used Naples biscuits, the foundation for many 18th- and 19th-century desserts, instead of sponge cakes, and syllabub instead of custard. It is very rich, so serve small portions.

300ml (½ pint) double cream
55g (2oz) caster sugar
2 tablespoons white wine
Grated rind of 1 lemon
12 sponge finger or boudoir
   biscuits
225g (8oz) redcurrant, quince or
   apple jelly
25g (1oz) chopped candied
   orange peel

Serves 6

Put the cream, sugar, wine and lemon rind into a large bowl and whisk until thick. Break the biscuits into several pieces and spoon layers of syllabub, biscuits and jelly alternately in an attractive glass bowl, ending with a layer of syllabub. Sprinkle with chopped candied orange peel and chill overnight.

Right: Whim-Wham
Next page: Lemon Posset

FLOATING ISLANDS

This elegant Georgian pudding, which is also very famous in France, consists of a rich custard covered with poached meringues – the floating islands.

600ml (1 pint) single cream

6 egg yolks

2 level teaspoons cornflour

175g (6oz) caster sugar

1 tablespoon rose-water

850ml (1½ pints) milk,
   for poaching

1 vanilla pod

4 egg whites

Pinch of salt

Crystallized rose petals

Toasted flaked almonds

Serves 6–8

Bring the cream gently to the boil in a heavy saucepan. Remove from the heat and cool a little. Cream the egg yolks, cornflour and 50g (1¾oz) sugar until almost white. Pour hot cream over the egg yolk mixture gradually, beating all the time. Rinse out the saucepan, leaving a film of cold water on the bottom. Return the custard to the saucepan and heat gently, stirring continuously until thick enough to coat the back of a wooden spoon (don't boil or the mixture will curdle). Remove from the heat and cool a little before stirring in the rose-water. Strain into a shallow serving bowl, sprinkle with sugar and leave to cool.

   To make the 'islands', fill a frying pan with milk, flavoured with a vanilla pod, and bring to simmering point. Whisk the egg whites with a pinch of salt until stiff peaks form. Whisk in 115g (4oz) caster sugar gradually, until smooth and shiny. Remove the vanilla pod from the pan. Using a tablespoon rinsed in cold water between each addition, spoon 4 islands into the pan of simmering water. Poach on each side for 2–3 minutes, until firm. Remove each island and drain on a clean towel. Repeat until the meringue mixture is used up (about 8 islands). Leave to cool. Arrange the islands on the 'lake' of custard and chill. To serve, sprinkle with crushed crystallized rose petals and toasted flaked almonds.

Left: Floating Islands
Previous page: Devonshire Junket

DEVONSHIRE JUNKET

This was a junket covered with clotted cream, popular in Devon and Cornwall – so simple, but so delicious. Junket has been made since the 13th century and is probably of Norman origin. Its name comes from the word jonquette, French for the little rush baskets in which it was made. The original junket was a rich confection of cream, curdled with rennet and flavoured with spices. Later, rose-water and orange-flower water were added and junket was eaten alongside the jellies and flummeries at the end of a meal.

600ml (1 pint) Jersey milk
or single cream
1 heaped tablespoon
    caster sugar
1 tablespoon brandy
Pinch of freshly grated nutmeg
    plus extra to garnish
1 level teaspoon rennet
Clotted cream and soft fruit
    to serve

Serves 4

Heat the milk or cream to 39°C (100°F). Stir in the sugar to dissolve it, followed by the brandy, nutmeg and rennet. Stir well, then pour into a glass bowl or 4 individual serving dishes and leave to set at room temperature (not in the refrigerator), for about 4 hours.

Chill in the refrigerator for about 1 hour before serving plain or sprinkled with grated nutmeg and accompanied by clotted cream and soft fruit or purée of raspberries or strawberries.

ORANGE AND LEMON JUNKET

This variation adds a fruity dimension.

ADDITIONAL INGREDIENT:
grated rind of 1 orange or
    lemon

Prepare the junket as instructed opposite but flavour the milk with the grated orange or lemon rind.

DAMASK CREAM

This version of junket was popular in 18th-century Bath.

ALTERNATIVE INGREDIENTS:
600ml (1 pint) single cream
4 tablespoons double or
    whipping cream
3 tablespoons rose-water
1 tablespoon caster sugar
Pink or red rose petals to
    decorate

Use single cream rather than milk to make the junket (as described opposite) and omit the brandy. Sprinkle with grated nutmeg. About 30 minutes before serving, mix together the double or whipping cream, the rose-water and the caster sugar. Pour this over the top of the junket. Serve with pink or red rose petals strewn over the top. Alternatively, mix 4 tablespoons of clotted cream with the rose-water and sugar and serve separately with the junket.

OLD-FASHIONED RICE PUDDING

In Georgian times a rice pudding could be a very elaborate dish. You can flavour your pudding with lemon or orange rind, ground cinnamon or nutmeg, half a vanilla pod (split lengthways), a few drops of rose-water, a few saffron threads or a fresh bay leaf. The important thing is to cook the rice very slowly if it is to achieve that unctuous richness and a buttery brown crust. If you have an Aga or similar stove, leave it in the lowest oven overnight, though you will need to add more milk.

55g (2oz) short-grain rice
850ml (1½ pints) full-cream milk
25g (1oz) butter, cut into little
    pieces
55g (2oz) caster sugar or 1 level
    tablespoon clear honey or
    golden syrup
Pinch of salt
1 curl of lemon rind
150ml (¼ pint) double cream
Freshly grated nutmeg

Serves 4–6

Put the rice, milk, butter, sugar, salt and lemon rind into a buttered ovenproof dish. Stir well, then add the cream. Stir again, then grate over plenty of nutmeg. Place uncovered in a preheated slow oven at 140°C, 275°F, gas mark 1 and cook for 3–4 hours, or until just starting to set. As the pudding cools, it will finish cooking in its own heat and thicken. Remove from the oven and leave until just warm, or cold, if you like.

Serve on its own, or with Jam, Syrup or Marmalade Sauce (see pages 92 and 93) or with stewed or fresh fruit.

VARIATIONS

Try adding 50g (1¾oz) chopped natural glacé cherries, candied peel, sultanas, currants or grated apple.

RICE PUDDING MERINGUE

Make a meringue topping with 2 egg whites and 115g (4oz) caster sugar. Pile on top of the rice pudding and return to the oven to brown the meringue.

RICE CREAMS

This delicate creamy pudding can be served with fresh soft fruit or any fruit sauce. It is basically a cold rice pudding, mixed with cream, but this description doesn't do it justice.

60g (2oz) short-grain rice
300ml (½ pint) full-cream milk
25g (1oz) caster sugar
1 vanilla pod
1 bay leaf
1 level teaspoon gelatine
2 eggs, separated
300ml (½ pint) double or
    whipping cream
Fern or strawberry leaves
    to garnish

Serves 4–6

Wash the rice in cold water, drain and put in a heavy saucepan with the milk, sugar, vanilla pod and bay leaf. Bring slowly to the boil, then cook over a gentle heat, stirring now and again to stop the rice sticking on the bottom of the pan, until tender, about 40–45 minutes.

Remove from the heat and take out the vanilla pod and bay leaf. Sprinkle the gelatine into the hot rice and stir until dissolved. Beat the egg yolks with 1 tablespoon of cream and stir into the rice. Return the pan to the heat for a few minutes, and then place in a bowl of cold water. Stir until cool, but not set.

Whip the remainder of the cream, until it begins to ribbon but does not stand in peaks. Whisk the egg whites until very stiff. Fold the cream into the cool rice, followed by the whipped egg whites. Pour into individual glasses and chill before serving. Decorate with a few raspberries or strawberries and place the glasses on saucers covered with a fern leaf or strawberry leaves.

QUEEN MAB'S PUDDING

This pudding is based on a recipe by Eliza Acton, from her Modern Cookery, *published in 1845. It is really a custard, set with gelatine, with candied fruits added to make it richer. Candying was a method of preserving fruit, popular in Tudor and Stuart days. Whole fruits were candied and served at the banquet course after the main meal, as well as being chopped and used in cakes, puddings and biscuits. If possible buy whole candied peel and chop it yourself.*

600ml (1 pint) full-cream milk
1 bay leaf
1 vanilla pod
Strip of lemon peel
2 large eggs, separated
40g (1½oz) caster sugar
2 tablespoons warm water
15g (½oz) gelatine
50g (1¾oz) chopped glacé
  cherries
25g (1oz) chopped candied
  citron or lemon peel

Serves 4–6

Put the milk, bay leaf, vanilla pod and lemon peel in a saucepan and bring slowly to the boil. Remove from the heat and cool a little. Beat egg yolks and sugar together and pour on the flavoured milk, stirring continuously. Remove the bay leaf, vanilla pod and lemon peel. Rinse the milk pan with cold water, leaving a film of water on the bottom, and return the milk and egg mixture to the pan. Heat gently, stirring all the time and cook until thick enough to coat the back of a wooden spoon. Remove from the heat.

Put warm water in a cup and sprinkle gelatine over the top. Place the cup in a pan of water and heat gently until the gelatine has dissolved. Pour through a warmed fine-mesh sieve into the custard. Whisk the egg whites very stiffly and fold into the cooled custard. Pour into a wetted mould and leave in a cool place until almost set. Stir in chopped cherries and peel and refrigerate to set completely.

Serve with a fruit sauce, such as Lemon Sauce (page 92) poured around the pudding.

OLD ENGLISH SHERRY TRIFLE

Trifles have an ancient history dating back to the Tudor and Stuart period, although they have changed in character over the years and this recipe belongs to the Victorian era.

1 fatless sponge cake made with
    3 eggs, 85g (3oz) caster sugar
    and 85g (3oz) plain flour or
    1 packet of trifle sponges
Good-quality apricot jam or
    apple or quince jelly
115g (4oz) ratafia biscuits
    or macaroons
About 6 tablespoons medium
    sherry or Madeira
2 tablespoons brandy (optional)
600ml (1 pint) single or
    double cream or milk
1 vanilla pod, split in half
    lengthways
50g (1¾oz) caster sugar
2 teaspoons cornflour
6 egg yolks
425ml (¾ pint) double or
    whipping cream
Icing sugar, to sweeten

Serves 6–8

Cut the sponge into 2.5cm (1in) slices and liberally spread with your chosen preserve. Arrange in a large glass bowl. Scatter over the ratafia biscuits, then sprinkle liberally with sherry or Madeira and brandy, if using.

To make the custard, bring the milk or cream with the vanilla pod to the boil. Mix the sugar with cornflour, add the egg yolks gradually and beat well until smooth. Remove the vanilla pod from the milk and pour on to the egg mixture, stirring all the time. Rinse out the milk pan, leaving a film of cold water in the bottom. Return the custard to the pan and stir well with a wooden spoon over a low heat until thick. Immediately the custard is thick enough, plunge the bottom of the pan into a bowl of cold water to stop the mixture curdling. Leave to cool a little.

When the custard is fairly cool, pour over the sponge, and leave to cool completely. When cool, whip the cream until it stands in peaks and spread a thick layer over the custard. Pipe the top with the remaining cream and decorate with lots of crystallized fruits, nuts and extra ratafias – the more the merrier, especially at Christmas. In the summer, the trifle looks lovely decorated with crystallized flowers, rose petals or fresh edible flowers.

TRINITY BURNT CREAM

Also known as Cambridge Cream or Trinity Pudding, this recipe is said to have been based on an ancient Scottish dish which may have been brought over from France by Mary, Queen of Scots. It is similar to the delicious French crème brûlée. The sugary top used to be browned by a 'salamander', a flat iron which was heated and passed over the top of the pudding. You can make this custard in one large baking dish or individual ovenproof dishes, and it is best made the day before you want to serve.

600ml (1 pint) double cream
1 vanilla pod split lengthways
5 egg yolks
1 tablespoon caster sugar
About 4 tablespoons
    demerara sugar
Edible flowers to decorate

Serves 4–6

In a saucepan, bring the cream with the vanilla pod very gently to the boil. Leave to cool a little, then remove the vanilla pod. Cream the egg yolks and sugar together in a basin until almost white. Pour the hot cream on to the yolks in a steady stream, whisking all the time. Strain into a shallow 700ml (1¼ pint) ovenproof dish and place in a roasting tin filled with enough hot water to come halfway up the sides of the dish. Cook in a preheated oven at 150°C, 300°F, gas mark 2 for 1–1¼ hours or until just set. Remove the dish from the oven and leave until cold. Chill in the refrigerator overnight, if possible. Just before serving, spread the demerara sugar in an even layer over the surface of the custard and spray with a little water (this helps caramelize). Heat a grill to its highest temperature, then place the pudding as near to the grill as possible until the sugar has melted and caramelized (if you have a chef's blowtorch, use this instead). Return the pudding to the refrigerator for 30 minutes before serving, decorated with a few edible flowers and accompanied by a bowl of fresh cherries, strawberries or raspberries in season.

FINE ALMOND BLANCMANGE

The English blancmange of the 18th century was a kind of jelly, stiffened with isinglass or hartshorn and flavoured with almonds and rose-water. By the early 1820s, arrowroot was being exported to Britain from the West Indies and became the thickening agent. Boiling milk, sweetened and seasoned with cinnamon, mace and lemon peel, was poured on to a solution of arrowroot. It was set in elaborate moulds – and here was the true forerunner of our modern cornflour blancmange.

40g (1½oz) cornflour
300ml (½ pint) milk
300ml (½ pint) single cream
1 bay leaf
Strip of lemon peel
2 tablespoons caster sugar
4–5 drops almond essence
25g (1oz) toasted flaked
    almonds

Serves 4–6

Mix the cornflour to a smooth paste with a little of the milk. Heat the rest of the milk and cream in a saucepan with the bay leaf and lemon peel and gradually blend in the cornflour mixture. Bring to simmering point and cook for about 3 minutes, stirring continuously until thickened. Remove from the heat and sweeten to taste. Stir in the almond essence. Pour into a fancy 600ml (1 pint) mould, rinsed out with cold water. Put in the refrigerator to set. Unmould on to a plate, decorate with toasted almonds and serve with fresh soft fruit or a fruit sauce, such as Lemon Sauce (page 92) and pouring cream or yoghurt.

CARAMEL PUDDING

This is a very elegant pudding that appeals to even the most jaded of appetites. The custard pudding is covered with a beautiful caramel sauce, and is delicious served with fresh strawberries or raspberries. Try flavouring with orange rind and juice instead of brandy.

115g (4oz) lump sugar
4 tablespoons cold water
1 teaspoon boiling water
600ml (1 pint) full-cream milk
1 vanilla pod
1 bay leaf
2 eggs
3 egg yolks
2 tablespoons caster sugar
1 tablespoon brandy (optional)

Serves 6

Preheat the oven to 160°C, 325°F, gas mark 3. Warm a 15cm (6in) soufflé dish or a 15cm (6in) cake tin or a fluted mould (this makes a very attractive pudding) in the oven. You can also use individual moulds, if preferred.

Put the sugar and cold water in a heavy-based saucepan. Heat gently until the sugar has dissolved. Bring to the boil and boil rapidly without stirring until a rich brown caramel is formed. Remove from the heat, add boiling water and pour into a warmed dish or mould. Using oven gloves or a tea towel, tip the mould carefully to coat the bottom and sides with hot caramel. Leave to get cold.

Heat the milk with the vanilla pod and bay leaf. Leave to stand for 30 minutes to infuse. Bring to the boil and remove the vanilla pod and bay leaf. Beat the eggs, egg yolks and sugar together until pale in colour. Pour the cooled milk on to the egg mixture a little at a time to avoid curdling the eggs, stirring continuously. Stir in the brandy, if using. Strain the custard into the prepared mould. Stand in a roasting tin half-filled with hot water and bake in the centre of a preheated oven for about 45 minutes (30 minutes for individual moulds) or until the custard is set. Cooking time will vary depending on the mould.

When cooked, remove the pudding from the oven, leave to cool completely and refrigerate before unmoulding. To unmould, loosen the edges of the pudding with the point of a knife. Place a shallow serving dish over the mould and turn out quickly. Serve chilled with soft fruit.

LITTLE CHOCOLATE POTS

This is one of those really rich chocolate mousses that chocoholics adore. Serve only a small quantity to each person. This recipe contains partially cooked eggs.

175g (6oz) good-quality
   plain chocolate
2 tablespoons water
15g (½oz) salted butter
3 eggs, separated

Serves 6

Break the chocolate into small pieces, then put in a basin with the water. Place over a pan of gently simmering water to melt the chocolate into a thick cream, stirring from time to time. Remove from the heat and stir in the butter. Beat in the egg yolks one at a time (they will be slightly cooked in the hot chocolate mixture). Leave to cool.

Whisk the egg whites until stiff, then briskly fold into the chocolate. When thoroughly mixed, pour into little custard pots or ramekins. Chill overnight.

Serve with homemade dessert biscuits.

VARIATIONS

LITTLE CHOCOLATE AND ORANGE POTS

Stir the grated rind of 1 large orange and 1 tablespoon of orange liqueur into the melted chocolate with the butter.

LITTLE CHOCOLATE AND COFFEE POTS

Stir 1 tablespoon of coffee essence or very strong espresso into the melted chocolate with the butter.

LONDON SYLLABUB

Syllabub is one of the oldest known British dishes. London Syllabub is one example of a typical Georgian syllabub of the 'everlasting' type, which meant that it didn't separate into a honeycombed curd on the top with an alcoholic drink underneath. Allow the lemon or orange rind and rosemary to infuse in the fruit juice and the alcohol, overnight if possible.

Finely pared rind of 1 lemon
   or 2 oranges
Juice of 1 lemon or orange
Sprig of fresh rosemary, bruised
150ml (¼ pint) white wine,
   dry sherry or Madeira
2 tablespoons brandy
85g (3oz) caster sugar or honey
300ml (½ pint) double cream
Sprigs of fresh rosemary for
   decorating

Serves 4–6

Put the lemon or orange rind and juice and rosemary in a bowl with the wine and brandy and leave overnight. Next day, strain the wine and orange or lemon mixture into a saucepan. Add the sugar or honey and heat gently until the sugar has dissolved. Pour into a large, deep bowl and leave to cool. Gradually stir in the cream, beating until it 'ribbons' and stands in soft peaks (don't use an electric blender or the cream may become grainy). Pour into individual glasses, or custard cups, and chill. Serve decorated with sprigs of rosemary.

LAVENDER OR GERANIUM SYLLABUB

Herbs and flowers can be used to add a fresh flavour to syllabub.

ALTERNATIVE INGREDIENT:
2 sprigs of lavender or
   8 lemon geranium leaves

Use the recipe opposite but flavour with the lavender, bruised well, instead of the rosemary. Serve decorated with lavender flowers. If using lemon geranium leaves instead, use 8 bruised leaves to 300ml (½ pint) cream.

SPICED SYLLABUB

This decadent syllabub is flavoured with spices.

ALTERNATIVE INGREDIENTS:
Finely pared rind of 1 orange
Finely pared rind of 1 lemon
1 stick of cinnamon
8 cloves
200ml (7fl oz) decent red wine

Infuse the orange rind, lemon rind, cinnamon stick and cloves in the wine overnight, then continue as described opposite. Serve decorated with orange zest.

ICE CREAMS

Iced Cream became popular in Britain in the 18th century with the development of ice houses on country estates. Large quantities of ice were stored in specially built brick or stone-lined pits to last the whole year, or more, if possible. When the winter was cold enough, this ice was taken from local ponds, lakes and rivers, otherwise it was brought from Scotland and Norway. Later, with better sea transport, ice came back in the holds of ships, as ballast, from North America.

The earliest ice creams were literally iced fruit creams or frozen fruit fools and were prepared in tall pewter pots with close-fitting lids, buried in pails filled with ice and salt. The first mechanical ice-cream maker was invented in the middle of the 19th century and made life a lot easier.

You can still make delicious ice cream by freezing fruit purée and cream, but by adding beaten eggs a lighter ice is produced which also softens more quickly for serving. It is great fun experimenting with ice creams and the possible variations, both simple and elaborate, seem endless. My favourite basic recipe was my mother-in-law's. She was a wonderful cook and a very special friend.

Don't worry if you haven't got an ice-cream maker – use a lidded plastic container instead and stir from time to time as the mixture freezes.

MARMALADE RIPPLE ICE CREAM

Any marmalade may be used in this recipe, depending on your personal taste, but top-quality thick-cut Seville is too strong except for the most dedicated marmalade lovers. Contains raw eggs.

4 large eggs, separated
1 tablespoon lemon juice
115g (4oz) caster sugar
425ml (¾ pint) double or whipping cream
4–8 tablespoons marmalade (to taste)
1 tablespoon orange liqueur

Serves 6–8

Beat the egg yolks with the lemon juice and caster sugar until pale and frothy. Whip the cream until it stands in soft peaks and add to the egg mixture. Whisk the egg whites until soft and fold gently into the mixture. Pour into a lidded plastic container and freeze. When the mixture is almost frozen, mix together the marmalade and orange liqueur, then fold into the ice cream to create a ripple effect.

Right: Marmalade Ripple Ice Cream
Next page: Ratafia Ice Cream

NESSELRODE PUDDING

This pudding was invented in the 19th century by Monsieur Mony, chef to the famous Count Nesselrode, after whom it was named. It is reputed to be the most famous of the iced puddings, and was always produced at Christmas. This particular recipe is based on one I found in an unusual recipe book called The Ice Book, *written in 1844 by Thomas Masters. If frozen in a fancy mould it would make a terrific alternative Christmas pudding. Contains partially cooked eggs.*

FOR THE VANILLA SYRUP
150ml (¼ pint) water
50g (1¾oz) granulated sugar
1 vanilla pod, split lengthways

FOR THE ICE CREAM
25g (1oz) candied peel, chopped
25g (1oz) raisins
25g (1oz) glacé cherries, quartered
25g (1oz) currants
2 egg yolks
50g (1¾oz) caster sugar
300ml (½ pint) single cream
225g (8oz) fresh or tinned
    unsweetened chestnut purée
1 tablespoon Maraschino liqueur
150ml (¼ pint) double or
whipping cream

Serves 6

Left: Nesselrode Pudding
Previous page: Chestnut Ice Cream

To make the vanilla syrup, bring the water, sugar and vanilla pod slowly to the bowl, stirring to dissolve the sugar. Boil rapidly for 5 minutes. Remove from the heat and cool. When completely cold, remove the vanilla pod. (This can be washed and used again, so it is not as expensive as it might seem.)

Poach the candied peel, raisins, cherries and currants in the vanilla syrup for a few minutes. Drain, reserving the syrup, and leave to cool.

Make a custard by beating egg yolks with the sugar until thick and pale yellow in colour. Heat the single cream to simmering point in a heavy-based saucepan, and stir into the egg mixture. Strain back into the saucepan and stir continuously over a gentle heat until the mixture thickens enough to coat the back of a spoon. Do not allow to boil. Pour into a large mixing bowl and leave to cool.

Mix the chestnut purée with the reserved vanilla syrup and add to the cooled custard with the Maraschino. Stir well and pour into a lidded container. Freeze for 1 hour and then remove. Whip the cream until it stands in soft peaks and add to the semi-set ice cream together with the prepared raisins and currants. Freeze again until firm.

Serve topped with vanilla-flavoured cream and decorate with crystallized violets and angelica. This pudding looks very attractive frozen in a mould, turned out and then decorated with piped cream and grated chocolate or glacé cherries, crystallized violets or apricots – make it as elaborate and decorative as you wish.

RATAFIA ICE CREAM

Small, elegant, button-shaped ratafia biscuits were an 18th-century favourite and make an excellent ice cream.

115g (4oz) ratafia biscuits
150ml (¼ pint) sweet sherry
4 eggs, separated
85g (3oz) caster sugar
425ml (¾ pint) double or whipping cream
25g (1oz) chopped toasted almonds

Serves 6–8

Crush the ratafia biscuits and soak them in sherry for 20 minutes. Beat the egg yolks and sugar until thick and pale yellow in colour. Whip the cream until it stands in peaks and add to the egg mixture. Fold in the soaked ratafia biscuits. Whisk the egg whites until stiff and fold into the mixture. Freeze in a lidded container for about 1 hour and then beat the mixture and add the chopped toasted almonds. Replace in the freezer and leave to set completely.

About 30 minutes before serving, move from the freezer into the refrigerator and leave to soften. Serve topped with seasonal soft fruit and cream.

CHESTNUT ICE CREAM

Years ago, chestnuts were grown and used in cooking much more than they are today. You will find this ice cream very delicate and unusual in flavour. Use fresh or tinned unsweetened chestnut purée. You can melt 85g (3oz) good-quality plain chocolate and add to the ice cream after the first stage of freezing, if preferred. Contains raw egg.

4 eggs, separated

115g (4oz) caster or soft
brown sugar

2–3 drops vanilla essence

225g (8oz) unsweetened
chestnut purée

450ml (16fl oz) double
or whipping cream

Marrons glacés to decorate
(optional)

FOR THE EASY CHOCOLATE
SAUCE

250g (9oz) good-quality plain
chocolate

2 tablespoons strong black
coffee, such as espresso

300ml (½ pint) whipping cream

Walnut-sized knob of butter

Serves 6–8

Beat the egg yolks with sugar and vanilla essence. Stir in the chestnut purée. Whip the cream until it stands in soft peaks and add to the chestnut mixture. Whisk the egg whites until stiff and fold gently into the mixture. Pour into a lidded container and freeze for about 1½ hours until mushy.

Remove the ice cream from the freezer and stir gently. Replace in the freezer and leave to freeze completely. Take the ice cream out of the freezer 30 minutes before you want to serve it, and leave in the refrigerator to soften and improve in flavour. Scoop into stemmed glasses, top with Easy Chocolate Sauce (see below) and decorate with marrons glacés, if desired. Particularly good at Christmas.

EASY CHOCOLATE SAUCE

Break the chocolate into small pieces and put into a heavy saucepan with the coffee and the cream. Heat slowly, stirring from time to time, until the chocolate has melted. Once the chocolate is softened, stir until smooth, then stir in the butter. Pour into a warm jug and serve. Suitable for pouring over poached pears, ice cream, chocolate pudding and meringues.

BLACKCURRANT ICE CREAM

This is an ice cream made using the custard method. Fresh or frozen berries, or homemade jam, sharpened with a squeeze of lemon – in which case omit the sugar – are successful. Any fruits can be used to make ice cream, but my favourites are damson, raspberry, a combination of rhubarb and redcurrant and blackberry as well as blackcurrant.

300ml (½ pint) double cream
300ml (½ pint) full-cream milk
4 eggs, separated
8 tablespoons caster sugar
450g (1lb) blackcurrants

Serves 6–8

Whisk the cream, milk, egg yolks and sugar together in a basin. Set over a pan of simmering water and continue whisking until the custard thickens enough to coat the spoon. Leave to cool.
Pick over the blackcurrants, if using fresh fruit, and remove any stalks. Liquidize the fruit to a thick purée and stir into the cooled custard.

Freeze the mixture until the edges are solid, but the middle is still soft – an hour or two. Beat the half-frozen mixture and fold in the egg whites, stiffly whisked. Freeze again until solid. Place in the refrigerator for 30 minutes before serving with thick cream.

LEMON MINT ICE CREAM

A refreshing ice cream which is ideal for a summer dinner party. Choose a good, strongly flavoured mint to ensure a balanced flavour. Contains raw eggs.

4 large eggs, separated
115g (4oz) caster sugar
300ml (½ pint) double cream
Grated rind and juice of
    2 large lemons
4 sprigs of strongly flavoured
    fresh mint

Serves 4–6

Whisk the egg whites until stiff, then whisk in the sugar a little at a time, until the mixture is light and stands in peaks. Beat the egg yolks until pale, then fold into the egg white until thoroughly mixed. Whip the cream with the lemon rind and juice and add to the egg mixture. Chop the mint finely and fold into the mixture, then turn into a lidded plastic container and freeze as usual.

ELDERFLOWER ICE CREAM

This creamy ice cream is very simple to make, particularly if you use a commercial elderflower cordial rather than making your own. This recipe contains raw egg whites.

2 large egg whites
1 tablespoon caster sugar
300ml (½ pint) double cream
90ml (3fl oz) good-quality
    elderflower cordial
Sprigs of elderflower, to
    decorate

Serves 4–6

Whisk the egg whites until stiff and beat in the sugar. Whip the cream until it stands in soft peaks, then beat in the elderflower cordial.

Fold the egg whites into the cream and turn the mixture into a lidded plastic container. Freeze for 4–5 hours until firm. Allow to soften in the refrigerator for 30 minutes before serving, scooped in stemmed glasses and decorated with elderflower, if in season.

STEM GINGER ICE CREAM

This is a delicious ice cream and ideal for serving at Christmas lunch as an alternative to Christmas pudding or as a refreshing alternative to Brandy Butter. It is very good served with meringues flavoured with ground ginger. Contains raw eggs.

4 eggs, separated

110g (4oz) caster sugar

1 teaspoon ground ginger

2 tablespoons brandy

425ml (¾ pint) double or
    whipping cream

6 large pieces stem ginger
    in syrup, chopped

Serves 6–8

Beat the egg yolks with the sugar, ground ginger and brandy. Whip the cream until it stands in soft peaks and add to the egg mixture. Whisk the egg whites until stiff and fold into the mixture. Pour into a lidded container and freeze for about 1 hour. Add 4 of the pieces of chopped stem ginger and stir evenly into semi-set ice cream. Return to the freezer until completely set.

Scoop into glasses, sprinkle with the remaining chopped ginger and pour over a little of the stem ginger syrup. Top with Easy Chocolate, Butterscotch or Ginger Sauce (see pages 67, 89 and 93).

HONEY AND BRANDY ICE CREAM

My mother-in-law gave me this recipe and it is one of my family's favourites. The brandy makes a softer ice cream which can be served from the freezer. Contains raw eggs.

4 large eggs, separated
115g (4oz) caster sugar
4 tablespoons clear honey,
    warmed
425ml (¾ pint) double cream
6 tablespoons brandy or cider
    brandy

Serves 6–8

Beat the egg yolks and sugar until pale in colour. Add the warmed honey a little at a time, beating continuously until pale and fluffy, then put to one side. Whisk the cream with the brandy until it forms soft peaks. Whisk the egg whites in a separate bowl until stiff. Pour the egg mixture into a large bowl, then fold in a quarter of the cream, followed by a quarter of the egg white. Repeat until all the cream and egg whites have been incorporated into the yolk mixture. Pour into a lidded plastic container and freeze in the usual way.

This recipe makes a softer ice cream than usual because of the alcohol content, so it can be served straight from the freezer.

Scoop into bowls or glasses and serve with Butterscotch or Coffee Sauce (see pages 89 and 90), or with a little poached seasonal fruit, such as rhubarb, gooseberries or plums.

BROWN-BREAD ICE CREAM

Introduced later in the 18th century than the fruit ice creams, brown-bread ice cream was not popular until late Victorian and Edwardian days, when it was served as a country weekend treat. The breadcrumbs can be fried, baked or grilled with the sugar. Contains raw eggs.

A little butter
85g (3oz) brown breadcrumbs
85g (3oz) soft dark brown sugar
3 large eggs, separated
½ tablespoon rum
300ml (½ pint) double cream
85g (3oz) icing sugar, sifted

Serves 4–6

Preheat the oven to 200°C, 400°F, gas mark 6. Grease a baking sheet with butter. In a bowl, mix together the breadcrumbs and sugar, then spread over the baking sheet. Bake for about 15 minutes until dark and caramelized, stirring now and again. Cool, then break up the crumbs with a fork.

Whisk the egg whites until stiff. Mix the egg yolks with the rum, then fold into the whites. Whisk the cream and icing sugar until floppy, then fold into the egg mixture, with the breadcrumbs.

Pour into a shallow plastic lidded container and freeze in the normal way, beating frequently as the mixture freezes.

Remove from the freezer to the refrigerator at least 30 minutes before serving with a hot or cold fruit sauce, such as damson, plum, blackcurrant or blackberry or Easy Chocolate Sauce (see page 67).

VANILLA ICE CREAM

If you want a vanilla ice cream with real flavour, this recipe is for you, but leave the vanilla pod whole if you prefer a more neutral-based ice cream.

1 vanilla pod
300ml (½ pint) full-cream milk
3 large egg yolks
About 115g (4oz) caster sugar
300ml (½ pint) double cream

Serves 6

Split the vanilla pod lengthways then, using a small knife, strip out the seeds on to a white plate, so that you don't lose any. Put the seeds on one side for later.

Put the milk and vanilla pod (without the seeds) into a saucepan. Bring slowly to the boil, stirring occasionally. Draw off the heat, cover and leave for 20 minutes to infuse.

Whisk the egg yolks in a bowl with the sugar and vanilla seeds, then whisk in the vanilla-infused milk including the pod. Set the bowl over a pan of gently simmering water and cook, stirring continuously, until the custard thickens and covers the back of a wooden spoon. Taste and add more sugar if you wish. Leave to cool, then strain.

Whip the cream lightly and fold into the custard, then pour into a lidded plastic container and freeze as usual.

Half an hour before serving, transfer to the refrigerator to soften.

VANILLA AND WALNUT ICE CREAM

This variation adds toasted walnuts to make a stunning ice cream.

ADDITIONAL INGREDIENT:
85g (3oz) chopped walnuts

Spread the chopped walnuts on to a baking tray and toast in a preheated oven at 200°C, 400°F, gas mark 6 for 4–7 minutes, shaking them once or twice. Tip into a metal sieve and shake to dislodge flakes of papery skin, which should be discarded. Leave to cool. When your ice cream is semi-frozen, fold in the toasted walnuts. Return to the freezer to set solid.

COLD PIES, TARTS AND FLANS

The British have been justly famous for their wonderful range of pies and tarts since the Middle Ages and many sweet recipes have hardly changed since then. There were raised and open pies, tarts, tartlets and pastries, and flans for which the pastry shell was baked blind, and the usual filling was a mixture of strained egg yolks, cream and various dried fruit and spices like our modern custard tarts. Cheese and almond tarts were also enjoyed as well as pies of apples, pears, figs and quinces, sweetened with honey.

In early times it was not easy to tell a savoury from a sweet pie, as nearly all included dried fruit and spices, and often fish pies were iced. Our modern mince pie is a hangover from these recipes, which began to go out of fashion in the eighteenth century.

The earliest forms of pastry were literally a paste of coarse flour and water or oil coating the fowl or fish and were discarded after cooking. The British began to use suet or fat and, later, butter to make their crusts, allowing for finer and more delicate pastry recipes to evolve. Really rich butter pastry or 'puff paste' was used in Elizabethan times to make fruit tarts and later jam tarts and patties.

The majority of the populace had to take their uncooked pastry items to communal ovens or pie-makers to be baked, as the equipment, space, fuel and technology were only available to the relatively well off.

RICH BAKEWELL PUDDING

The original Bakewell Pudding recipe was made in a special oval tin and had a thick layer of preserved fruit, such as peaches or apricots, and strips of candied citron or orange peel spread over the pastry. A custard made with eggs, butter and sugar and flavoured with what the Bakewellians call 'lemon brandy' (brandy flavoured with lemon rind) was poured on top and the pudding was baked. Ratafia or almond flavouring is more commonly used now, and flaky pastry can be used instead of shortcrust.

175g (6oz) shortcrust pastry
(see page 10)
3 heaped tablespoons
homemade or good-quality
apricot jam
25g (1oz) candied peel, chopped
3 eggs
115g (4oz) caster sugar
115g (4oz) unsalted butter
½ teaspoon vanilla extract or
ratafia flavouring
1 tablespoon brandy
115g (4oz) ground almonds
Sieved icing sugar for sprinkling

Serves 6

Roll out the pastry and use to line a buttered 20cm (8in) oval pie dish. Chill, then bake blind in the usual way (see Apricot Amber Pudding, page 23). Spread the jam evenly over the cooled pastry case and sprinkle with the peel.

Beat the eggs and sugar together until pale and thick. Melt the butter and run into the egg mixture. Beat together well. Stir in vanilla essence or ratafia and brandy. Fold in the ground almonds. Pour the mixture over the jam and candied peel in the pastry case. Bake in the centre of a preheated oven at 180°C, 350°F, gas mark 4, for about 30 minutes or until the filling is set and golden brown. Dust with sieved icing sugar and serve hot, warm or cold with pouring cream.

VARIATION
ALDERMAN'S PUDDING
A popular pudding in the south of England using apricot jam, but no candied peel or brandy.

WALNUT AND HONEY TART

Walnuts have been grown in Britain for centuries. Villagers used to gather them in the autumn and make them into pies, puddings, sauces, cakes, soups and stuffings. They were also added to meat and fish dishes and pickled. This traditional tart is very rich, so serve in small portions.

175g (6oz) shortcrust pastry
   (see page 10)
85g (3oz) butter
125g (4½oz) soft brown sugar
Grated rind of 1 orange
3 eggs
175g (6oz) clear honey
A few drops of vanilla essence
110g (4oz) broken walnuts
Walnut halves for decorating

Serves 6–8

Roll out chilled pastry and use to line a 20cm (8in) flan ring. Bake blind in the usual way (see Apricot Amber Pudding, page 23).

Cream the butter, gradually adding the sugar and the orange rind. Beat until well blended, then beat the eggs and add gradually to the creamed mixture, beating continuously. Add the honey and vanilla essence, mixing to a smooth consistency. Stir in the broken walnuts, then pour into the pastry case. Arrange walnut halves on top, then bake in the centre of a preheated oven at 200°C, 400°F, gas mark 6 for about 40 minutes, or until set. Protect the top with foil if it is browning too quickly.

Remove from the oven and leave to cool, then serve with plenty of chilled cream.

CHOCOLATE AND PRUNE TART

Chocolate was introduced into Britain in the mid-17th century from Mexico, where the Aztecs had mixed it with honey. It remained a luxury drink as long as the price of sugar was high, and was never as popular as coffee or tea. A pie with a chocolate filling like this would have been considered a great luxury.

FOR THE SWEET
   SHORTCRUST PASTRY
175g (6oz) plain flour
Pinch of salt
85g (3oz) icing sugar
150g (5½oz) unsalted butter
2 small egg yolks, beaten

FOR THE PRUNE PUREE
300g (10oz) ready-to-eat prunes
2 tablespoons brandy

FOR THE CHOCOLATE
   FILLING
100g (3½oz) good-quality plain
   chocolate (72% cocoa fat)
2 eggs, separated
300ml (½ pint) double cream
85g (3oz) caster sugar
Sifted icing sugar, to dust

Serves 8–10

To make the pastry, sieve the flour with the salt and icing sugar into a bowl. Rub in the butter, then mix to a soft dough with the egg yolks. Knead very briefly, then wrap in clingfilm and chill in the refrigerator for 30 minutes. Roll out and use to line a buttered 25cm (10in) flan tin. Bake blind in the usual way (see page 23).

Meanwhile, make the prune purée by simmering the stoned prunes gently, with barely enough water to cover, for 5–10 minutes or until very tender. Lift them out with a slotted spoon and process with the brandy and just enough of the juice to make a thick purée (about 3 tablespoonfuls). Spread over the base of the pastry case.

To make the filling, break the chocolate into pieces and place in a bowl set over a pan of gently simmering water, making sure that the base of the bowl does not come into contact with the water. Remove the bowl as soon as the chocolate has melted and cool slightly, then beat in the egg yolks one by one. Lightly whip the cream and fold into the chocolate mixture. Whisk the egg whites until they form soft peaks, then sprinkle over the sugar and continue to whisk until glossy. Fold into the chocolate mixture, then pour into the pastry case.

Bake in a preheated oven at 200°C, 400°F, gas mark 6, for about 40–50 minutes until puffed and set around the edges, but still wobbly in the centre. Serve warm or cold dusted with icing sugar and with Vanilla Ice Cream, Orange Cream Sauce (see pages 74 and 91), or the cream of your choice.

Right: Chocolate and Prune Tart

LEMON MERINGUE PIE

A classic British pudding which most people love. It is a brilliant mixture of white foaming meringue and contrasting tangy lemon filling.

FOR THE PASTRY

175g (6oz) plain flour
1 tablespoon icing sugar
115g (4oz) cold butter, cut into
small pieces
1 egg yolk
1 tablespoon ice-cold water

FOR THE FILLING

115g (4oz) caster sugar
2 level tablespoons cornflour
Grated rind of 2 large lemons
125ml (4fl oz) lemon juice
Juice of 1 small orange
85g (3oz) butter, cut into
small pieces
3 egg yolks
1 whole egg

FOR THE MERINGUE

4 egg whites
225g (8oz) caster sugar
2 level teaspoons cornflour

Right: Lemon Meringue Pie

To make the pastry, sieve the flour and icing sugar into a mixing bowl. Rub in the butter, then add the egg yolk and enough water to mix to a dough. Roll out and line a buttered 23cm (9in) flan tin. Prick the base with a fork, line with foil and chill for 30 minutes to 1 hour or overnight. Put a baking sheet in the oven and preheat to 200°C, 400°F, gas mark 6. Bake blind in the usual way (see page 23). Remove from the oven and set aside. Lower the oven to 180°C, 350°F, gas mark 4.

To make the filling, mix the sugar, cornflour and lemon rind in a saucepan. Strain and gradually stir in the lemon juice. Make the orange juice up to 200ml (7fl oz) with water and strain into the pan. Cook over a medium heat, stirring, until thick and smooth. Once the mixture bubbles, remove from the heat and beat in the butter until melted. Beat the egg yolks and whole egg together, then add to the pan and return to the heat. Stir until the mixture thickens. Remove from the heat.

Whisk the egg whites to soft peaks, then add half the sugar, a spoonful at a time, whisking between each addition without overbeating. Whisk in the cornflour, then add the rest of the sugar until smooth and glossy. Reheat the filling and pour it into the pastry case. Pile spoonfuls of meringue around the edge of the filling, then spread so it just touches the pastry. Pile the remaining meringue into the centre, spreading so that it touches the surface of the hot filling and starts to cook, then give it all a swirl. Return to the oven for 18–20 minutes until the meringue is crisp.

Remove from the oven and leave in the tin for 30 minutes, then remove and leave for another 30 minutes to 1 hour before serving.

RICHMOND MAIDS OF HONOUR

Similar recipes go back to the Middle Ages, but these particular little almond-flavoured curd tarts were great favourites at the court of Henry VIII in Richmond Palace, particularly with Anne Boleyn. Henry is said to have named them after her when he saw her eating them while she was maid of honour to Catherine of Aragon, his first wife. Puff pastry is traditional, but rich shortcrust is suitable too.

225g (8oz) puff pastry
(see page 11)
2 tablespoons quince or apple
jelly or apricot jam

FOR THE FILLING
225g (8oz) curd or
cottage cheese
85g (3oz) caster sugar
Grated rind of 1 lemon
50g (1¾oz) ground almonds
2 eggs
1 tablespoon brandy (optional)
Icing sugar, for dusting

Makes about 18

Grease some patty or tartlet tins. Roll out the pastry very thinly and, using an 8cm (3¼in) cutter, cut out rounds of pastry to line the tins. Spoon a little jelly or jam into the bottom of each pastry case. Chill while you prepare the filling.

Sieve the curd or cottage cheese into a bowl and mix in the caster sugar, lemon rind and ground almonds. Beat the eggs, add the brandy if using, and add to the curd mixture. Mix very thoroughly until well blended. Fill each pastry case two-thirds full with the cheese mixture. Bake in the centre of a preheated oven at 200°C, 400°F, gas mark 6 for about 25 minutes or until well risen and puffy. Serve warm or cold, dusted with sieved icing sugar and with clotted or pouring cream.

YORKSHIRE CURD CHEESECAKE

This variation on Maids of Honour is made as one big tart, instead of individual ones, and uses rich shortcrust instead of puffed pastry.

ALTERNATIVE INGREDIENTS:
225g (8oz) rich shortcrust
   pastry (see page 10)
1 tablespoon currants or raisins

Make one large tart rather than individual ones, as before, using rich shortcrust instead of puff pastry. Omit the jelly or jam, but add the currants or raisins to the cheese mixture, leaving out 25g (1oz) caster sugar. Bake for 30–40 minutes or until the filling is golden brown and puffy.

ORANGE-FLOWER CHEESE TART

Cheesecakes were originally baked in a pastry case, but I prefer a biscuit crumb base. However, do try both and see which you like. Orange-flower water was substituted for rose-water in some English dishes towards the end of the 17th century. Few English gardens had fallen orange blossoms to make this scented water, so it was usually imported from France or Portugal. Both orange-flower and rose-water continued in popularity as food flavourings all through the 18th century, but then lost favour. Recently, there has been a renewed interest and they can be bought at grocers or chemists. Cream cheese has been made in Britain since Roman times and a cheesecake of a similar recipe dates back to the 17th century. It is not, as some people may imagine, a modern invention from North America. Bake this tart the day before serving.

225g (8oz) digestive biscuits
225g (8oz) butter
700g (1lb 9oz) cream cheese
225g (8oz) caster sugar
3 eggs
1 teaspoon orange-flower water
1 level tablespoon grated
   orange rind
150ml (¼ pint) soured cream
Fresh orange slices, for
   decorating

Serves 12

Put the biscuits in a plastic bag and crush with a rolling pin. Melt 115g (4oz) butter and mix together with the biscuit crumbs in a mixing bowl. Press into a 23cm (9in) spring-release cake tin to cover the base. Refrigerate while making the filling.

In a large mixing bowl, beat the cream cheese until smooth. Slowly beat in sugar until evenly blended. Add the remaining butter, melted in a small saucepan, and the beaten eggs, orange-flower water and grated orange rind. Continue beating until the mixture is really smooth. Pour into the chilled crumb base. Bake in the centre of a preheated oven at 150°C, 300°F, gas mark 2 for 45 minutes. Turn off the oven, but leave the cheesecake in the oven for a further 30 minutes. Remove from the oven and cool. Leave in a cool place, overnight if possible.

To serve, remove the sides of the tin and loosen the cheesecake from the base with a palette knife. Slide it on to a plate and spread the top with soured cream. Decorate with fresh orange twists.

FRUIT-TOPPED CHEESECAKE

This variation on the cheese tart opposite gives a delicious fruity cheesecake.

ADDITIONAL INGREDIENTS:
fresh redcurrants, raspberries,
   strawberries, cranberries,
   rhubarb, cherries,
   blackcurrants or blackberries

Make the cheese tart as before but top with the fresh fruit. Glaze if you wish with melted redcurrant or apple jelly.

A SWEET EGG PIE

Also known as Custard Tart and Transparent Pudding, this pie has been popular since Elizabethan days when the filling was made with vegetables or fruit, eggs, thick cream and lots of spices. Originally the pastry case was literally to provide a 'coffyn' or container in which to cook the custard.

175g (6oz) sweet shortcrust
    pastry (see Chocolate and
    Prune Tart, page 80)
500ml (18fl oz) whipping cream
1 vanilla pod, split in half
    lengthways
6 egg yolks
85g (3oz) caster sugar
1 teaspoon cornflour
1 teaspoon rose-water
    (optional)
Freshly grated nutmeg

Serves 4–6

Roll out the pastry and use to line a buttered 20cm (8in), 5cm (2in) deep flan ring. Bake blind in the usual way (see Apricot Amber Pudding, page 23). Reduce the heat to 150°C, 300°F, gas mark 2.

Meanwhile make the custard filling by pouring the cream into a small pan. Add the vanilla pod and bring to the boil. Beat the egg yolks, sugar and cornflour together, then pour on the boiling cream. Stir well, then add the rose-water. Pass through a fine sieve, skimming any froth from the surface. Pour the custard mixture into the baked pastry case, grating plenty of fresh nutmeg across the surface. Place carefully in the oven and cook for about 30 minutes, or until just set (gently shake the baking tray – a slight wobble will indicate that the tart is cooked).

Remove from the oven and allow to cool to room temperature, before serving dusted with icing sugar. Eat with fresh soft fruit or a sauce, or serve plain (don't put in the refrigerator or the texture will firm up and spoil).

MANCHESTER TART

Also called Manchester Pudding, as its original form in the 18th century would have been made in a deep pie dish lined around the side with pastry. When Queen Victoria made a royal visit to Manchester, this humble, everyday local pudding was glamorised for her visit with the addition of a meringue topping.

175g (6oz) shortcrust pastry

FOR THE FILLING
300ml (½ pint) full-cream milk
Grated rind of 1 lemon
50g (1¾oz) fresh white
    breadcrumbs
2 large eggs, separated
50g (1¾oz) butter, melted
1 tablespoon brandy
100g (3½oz) caster sugar
3 tablespoons good-quality jam
    of your choice

Serves 6

Roll out the pastry and use to line a buttered 20cm (8in) pie plate or shallow flan tin. Bake blind in the usual way (see Apricot Amber Pudding, page 23).

To make the filling, bring the milk to the boil in a pan with the lemon rind. Remove from the heat and allow to cool so that the flavour of the lemon will infuse with the milk. Pour the cooled milk through a sieve over the breadcrumbs. Beat the egg yolks into the mixture, then add the melted butter, brandy and 25g (1oz) of the sugar. Spread your chosen jam into the pastry case and pour over the filling.

Bake in a preheated oven at 180°C, 350°F, gas mark 4 for 40–45 minutes. While the tart is cooking, whisk the egg whites with half the remaining sugar until stiff, then fold in the rest of the sugar. Coat the top of the tart with this meringue, then put it back in the oven for about 15 minutes until crisp and lightly browned.

SAUCES

CARAMEL SAUCE

150g (5½oz) caster sugar
100ml (3½fl oz) water
200ml (7fl oz) single cream
100g (3½oz) salted butter

Dissolve the sugar in the water in a saucepan. Do not stir. Put the pan on a moderate heat and let it bubble away until it reaches a rich amber colour. Add the cream and take off the heat. Whip in the butter and pour around a baked apple or over ice cream.

If you want it thicker, use double or whipping cream instead of the single variety.

BUTTERSCOTCH SAUCE

60g (2oz) butter
150g (5½oz) demerara sugar
1 tablespoon golden syrup
150g (5½oz) evaporated milk

Melt the butter, then add the sugar and syrup. Stir until dissolved, then pour in the evaporated milk. Turn up the heat and beat until boiling. Serve hot.

COFFEE SAUCE

115g (4oz) demerara sugar
2 tablespoons water
300ml (½ pint) strong
    black coffee
2 tablespoons Tia Maria

Dissolve the sugar in the water by heating gently in a saucepan. When the sugar has dissolved, boil rapidly until the syrup becomes golden. Add the coffee and Tia Maria. Boil for a few minutes until syrupy.

CHOCOLATE AND COFFEE SAUCE

115g (4oz) good-quality plain
    chocolate, broken into pieces
3 tablespoons strong
    black coffee
50g (1¾oz) unsalted butter

Put the chocolate and coffee into the top of a double saucepan and stir over the heat until the chocolate has melted. Beat in the butter gradually until the sauce is smooth and glossy.

CHOCOLATE ORANGE SAUCE

350ml (12fl oz) water
115g (4oz) caster sugar
1½ tablespoons cornflour
25g (1oz) cocoa powder
1 tablespoon instant coffee
  granules
50g (1¾oz) good-quality
  dark chocolate
2 strips of orange zest
Grand Marnier to taste

This easy sauce can be stored in the refrigerator for 4 weeks to use on ice cream or any pudding whenever you fancy. Combine 200ml (7fl oz) water and the sugar in a saucepan. Bring to the boil, stirring occasionally to dissolve the sugar. In a bowl, mix the remaining water with the cornflour and cocoa powder. When the sugar syrup is boiling, stir the cocoa mixture again and then pour it into the pan. Whisk very well, then simmer for 5 minutes. Add the coffee, chocolate and orange zest and stir until smooth. Remove from the heat, cover and leave to cool completely. When the sauce is cold, strain it and flavour to taste with the liqueur. Pour the sauce into a jar, cover and store in the refrigerator until needed.

ORANGE CREAM SAUCE

600ml (1 pint) double cream
1 tablespoon caster sugar
Grated rind and juice of
  2 oranges

Simmer the cream and sugar together in a large saucepan for about 45 minutes, or until it has reduced by half. Stir in the orange rind and juice and serve.

LEMON SAUCE

4 tablespoons homemade
    lemon curd
150ml (¼ pint) single cream

Mix the lemon curd and cream together. Heat in a saucepan over a low heat until hot but not boiling. Serve in a warmed jug.

JAM SAUCE

3 tablespoons raspberry,
    strawberry, plum, apricot
    or blackcurrant jam
6 tablespoons water
1 teaspoon lemon juice

Melt the jam in a saucepan with the water and lemon juice. Push through a sieve to make a smooth sauce. Serve hot.

SYRUP SAUCE

4 tablespoons golden syrup
2 tablespoons water
Juice of ½ lemon

Simmer the syrup and water together in a small saucepan for 2–3 minutes. Add the lemon juice and serve hot.

MARMALADE SAUCE

1 level teaspoon cornflour
Juice of 1 orange
300ml (½ pint) white wine
4 heaped tablespoons
    marmalade
2 tablespoons soft brown sugar

Dissolve the cornflour in the orange juice. Heat the wine, marmalade and sugar in a saucepan until the sugar has dissolved, stirring from time to time. Stir in the cornflower mixture and bring to the boil, stirring well. Simmer for 2 minutes. Serve hot.

GINGER SAUCE

2 pieces preserved stem ginger
1 tablespoon caster sugar
1 tablespoon dark rum
150ml (¼ pint) double cream

Chop the ginger very finely. Mix with sugar and rum. Stir in the double cream and continue stirring until thick. Chill before serving.

BRANDY AND LEMON BUTTER

115g (4oz) butter
115g (4oz) caster sugar
½ teaspoon grated lemon rind
1 tablespoon boiling water
1 teaspoon lemon juice
4 tablespoons brandy
Grated lemon rind for
    decoration

Cut the butter into small pieces and put with the sugar and lemon rind in a warmed bowl. Beat until creamy. Add the boiling water and continue to beat until every grain of sugar has dissolved (this will prevent the sauce from developing a gritty texture). Add lemon juice and brandy a little at a time, beating continuously to stop the sauce curdling. When completely blended, put in an attractive dish and store in the refrigerator until needed. Serve sprinkled with grated lemon rind.

RUM AND ORANGE BUTTER

115g (4oz) butter
115g (4oz) caster sugar
½ teaspoon grated orange rind
1 tablespoon boiling water
1 teaspoon orange juice
4 tablespoons rum
Grated orange rind for
    decoration

Make exactly as Brandy and Lemon Butter, substituting orange rind and juice for lemon, and rum for brandy. Serve chilled, sprinkled with grated orange rind.

SENIOR WRANGLER SAUCE

115g (4oz) butter
115g (4oz) caster sugar
50g (2oz) ground almonds
1 tablespoon boiling water
4 tablespoons brandy
a few drops of almond essence

Cut the butter into small pieces and put with sugar in a warmed bowl. Beat until creamy. Add the ground almonds and boiling water and continue to beat until every grain of sugar has dissolved. Gradually add brandy and almond essence, beating continuously. Serve very cold with rich fruit, steamed and plain sponge puddings.

VANILLA CUSTARD SAUCE

6 large egg yolks
70g (2½oz) caster sugar
1 vanilla pod
300ml (½ pint) full-cream milk
300ml (½ pint) double cream

Beat the egg yolks and sugar together in a bowl until well blended. Split and scrape the seeds of the vanilla pod into a pan with the milk and cream and bring to the boil. Place the bowl containing the egg-yolk mixture over a pan of hot water and whisk the cream into the mixture. As the egg yolks warm, the cream will thicken to create a custard. Keep stirring until it coats the back of a spoon. Remove the bowl from the heat and serve warm or cold.

INDEX

Alderman's Pudding 78
Almond
  Apple and Almond
    Pudding 35
  Bakewell Pudding, Rich 78
  Edinburgh Fog 29
  Fine Blancmange 57
  Flummery 17
  Lemon Solid 18
  Ratafia Ice Cream 66
  Richmond Maids of
    Honour 82
  Senior Wrangler Sauce 95
Apple
  and Almond Pudding 35
  Black Caps 37
  and Brandy Trifle 33
  Iced Apples 37
  and Marmalade Pudding 35
  Mother Eve's Pudding 34
  Spiced Winter Pudding 31
  Victorian Apple Snow 36
Apricot
  Alderman's Pudding 78
  Amber Pudding 23
  Bakewell Pudding, Rich 78
  Richmond Maids of
    Honour 82
  Spiced Winter Pudding 31

Bakewell Pudding, Rich 78
Blackberry
  Summer Pudding 30
Black Caps 37
Blackcurrant
  Ice Cream 68
  Summer Pudding 30
Boodles Orange Fool 15
Brandied Peaches 42
Brandy and Lemon Butter
  94
Bread
  Spiced Winter Pudding 31
  Summer Pudding 30
Brown-Bread Ice Cream 73
Butter'd Oranges 14
Butterscotch Sauce 89

Caramel
  Floating Islands 49
  Pudding 58
  Sauce 89
  Trinity Burnt Cream 56
Cherries in Red Wine 21
Chestnut
  Ice Cream 67
  Nesselrode Pudding 58
Chocolate
  and Coffee Pots, Little 59
  and Orange Pots, Little 59
  Orange Sauce 91
  and Prune Tart 80
  Pots, Little 59
  Sauce, Easy 67
Clare College Mush 32
Coffee
  and Chocolate Pots, Little
    59
  Sauce 90
Cranachan 26
Creamy Nectarine Tart 43
Custard Sauce, Vanilla 95
Custard Tart 86

Damask Cream 51
Damson Snow 28
Dates
  Black Caps 37
Devonshire Junket 50

Edinburgh Fog 29
Elderflower
  Ice Cream 70
  Trifle 46
Excellent Lemon Pudding,
  An 19

Fine Almond Blancmange
  57
Fine Orange Flummery 16
Fine Orange and Madeira
  Flummery 17
Floating Islands 49
Fruit-topped Cheesecake
  85

Ginger
  Ice Cream 71
  Sauce 93
Gooseberry
  and Elderflower Fool 39
  Tansy 41
  Trifle, Mrs Beeton's 40
Honey
  and Brandy Ice Cream 72
  Walnut and Honey Tart 79

Iced Apples 37

Jam
  Manchester Tart 87
  Sauce 92
Jelly
  Moonshine 20
  Port Wine 27
  Rhubarb and Red Wine 25
Junket
  Devonshire 50
  Lemon 51
  Orange 51

Lavender Syllabub 61
Lemon
  and Brandy Butter 94
  Junket 51
  Meringue Pie 81
  Mint Ice Cream 69
  Moonshine 20
  Posset 47
  Pudding, An Excellent
    Lemon 19
  Sauce 92
  Solid 18
Little Chocolate Pots 59
Little Chocolate and Orange
  Pots 59
Little Chocolate and Coffee
  Pots 59
London Syllabub 60

Manchester Tart 87
Marmalade Ripple Ice Cream
  64
Marmalade Sauce 93

Meringue
  Clare College Mush 32
  Lemon Meringue Pie 81
  Manchester Tart 87
  Rice Pudding Meringue 52
Moonshine 20
Mother Eve's Pudding 34

Nectarines Baked in Cream
  43
Nectarine Tart, Creamy 43
Nesselrode Pudding 65
Old English Sherry Trifle 55
Old-fashioned Rice Pudding
  52
Orange
  Butter'd 14
  and Chocolate Pots 59
  Cream Sauce 91
  Flummery, Fine Orange 16
  Fool, Boodles 14
  Junket 51
  London Syllabub 60
  and Madeira Flummery,
    Fine 17
  Posset 47
  and Rhubarb Fool 24
  and Rum Butter 55
Orange-flower Cheese
  Tart 84

Pastry
  Puff Pastry 11
  Rich Shortcrust Pastry 10
  Shortcrust Pastry 10
Pears
  Spiced in Red Wine 38
Plums in Sloe Gin 22
Port Wine Jelly 27
Posset, Lemon 47
Posset, Orange 47
Prune and Chocolate Tart 80

Queen Mab's Pudding 54

Raspberry
  Clare College Mush 32
  Cranachan 26
  Summer Pudding 30

Ratafia Ice Cream 66
Red Wine, Cherries in 21
Rhubarb
  and Orange Fool 24
  and Red Wine Jelly 25
Rice
  Creams 53
  Pudding, Old-Fashioned 52
Rich Bakewell Pudding 78
Richmond Maids of Honour
  82
Rum and Orange Butter 94

Senior Wrangler Sauce 95
Spiced Pears in Red Wine 38
Spiced Winter Pudding 31
Stem Ginger Ice Cream 71
Strawberry
  Clare College Mush 32
  Summer Pudding 30
Summer Pudding 30
Sweet Egg Pie 86
Syllabub
  Geranium Syllabub 61
  Lavender Syllabub 61
  London Syllabub 60
  Spiced Syllabub 61
Syrup Sauce 92

Trifle
  Apple and Brandy 33
  Elderflower 46
  Gooseberry, Mrs Beeton's
    40
  Sherry Trifle, Old English 55
  Whim-wham 48
Trinity Burnt Cream 56

Vanilla Custard Sauce 95
Vanilla Ice Cream 74
Victorian Apple Snow 36

Walnut
  and Honey Tart 79
  and Vanilla Ice Cream 75
Whim-Wham 48

Yorkshire Curd Cheesecake
  83

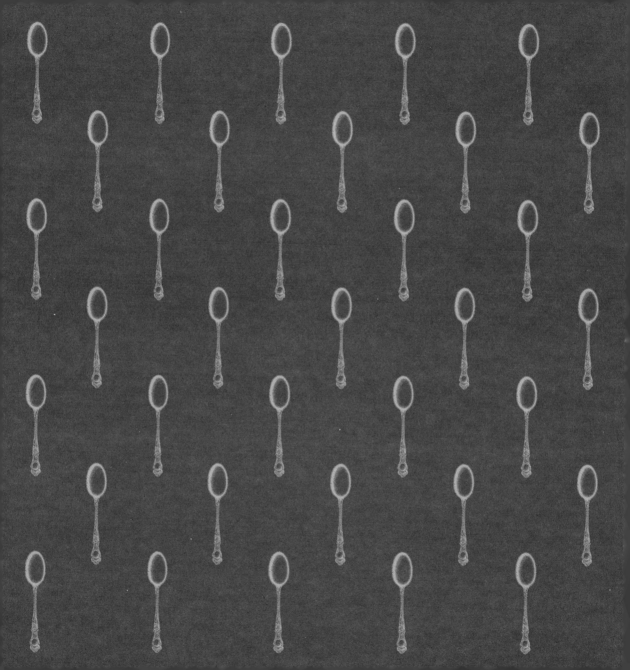